34.95

BARRIERS, DEFENCES AND RESISTANCE

Core concepts in therapy

Series Editor: Michael Jacobs

Over the last ten years a significant shift has taken place in the relations between representatives of different schools of therapy. Instead of the competitive and often hostile reactions we once expected from each other, therapists from different points of the spectrum of approaches are much more interested in where they overlap and where they differ. There is a new sense of openness to cross orientation learning.

The Core Concepts in Therapy series compares and contrasts the use of similar terms across a range of the therapeutic models, and seeks to identify where different terms appear to denote similar concepts. Each book is authored by two therapists, each one from a distinctly different orientation; and where possible each one from a different continent, so that an international dimension becomes a feature of this network of ideas.

Each of these short volumes examines a key concept in psychological therapy, setting out comparative positions in a spirit of free and critical enquiry, but without the need to prove one model superior to another. The books are fully referenced and point beyond themselves to the wider literature on each topic.

List of forthcoming and published titles:
Barden & Stimpson: *Words and Symbols*
Dilys Davies & Dinesh Bhugra: *Models of Psychopathology*
Paul Brinich & Christopher Shelley: *The Self and Personality Structure*
Dawn Freshwater & Chris Robertson: *Emotions and Needs*
Jan Grant & Jim Crawley: *Transference and Projection*
Richard J. Hazler & Nick Barwick: *The Therapeutic Environment*
David Edwards & Michael Jacobs: *Conscious and Unconscious*
John Davy and Malcolm Cross: *Barriers, Defences and Resistance*
John Rowan & Michael Jacobs: *The Therapist's Use of Self*
Lynn Seiser & Colin Wastell: *Interventions and Techniques*
Gabrielle Syme & Jenifer Elton-Wilson: *Objectives and Outcomes*
Val Simanowitz & Peter Pearce: *Personality Development*
Nick Totton & Michael Jacobs: *Character and Personality Types*
Kenneth C. Wallis & James L. Poulton: *Internalization*

BARRIERS, DEFENCES AND RESISTANCE

John Davy
and
Malcolm Cross

Open University Press

Open University Press
McGraw-Hill Education
McGraw-Hill House
Shoppenhangers Road
Maidenhead
Berkshire
England
SL6 2QL

email: enquiries@openup.co.uk.
world wide web: www.openup.co.uk

and Two Penn Plaza, New York, NY 10121-2289, USA

First published 2004

A catalogue record of this book is available from the British Library

ISBN 0 335 20886 X (pb) 0 335 20887 8 (hb)

Library of Congress Cataloging-in-Publication Data
CIP data has been applied for

Typeset by RefineCatch Limited, Bungay, Suffolk
Printed in the UK by Bell & Bain Ltd, Glasgow

Contents

Series editor's preface

A major aspect of intellectual and cultural life in the twentieth century has been the study of psychology – present of course for many centuries in practical form and expression in the wisdom and insight to be found in spirituality, in literature and in the dramatic arts, as well as in arts of healing and guidance, in both the East and West. In parallel with the deepening interest in the inner processes of character and relationships in the novel and theatre in the nineteenth century, psychiatry reformulated its understanding of the human mind, and encouraged, in those brave enough to challenge the myths of mental illness, new methods of exploration of psychological processes.

The twentieth century witnessed, especially in its latter half, an explosion of interest both in theories about personality, psychological development, cognition and behaviour, and in the practice of therapy, or perhaps more accurately, the therapies. It also saw, as is not uncommon in any intellectual discipline, battles between theories and therapists of different persuasions, particularly between psychoanalysis and behavioural psychology, and each in turn with humanistic and transpersonal therapies, and also within the major schools themselves. If such arguments are not surprising, and indeed objectively can be seen as healthy – potentially promoting greater precision in research, alternative approaches to apparently intractable problems and deeper understanding of the wellsprings of human thought, emotion and behaviour – it is none the less disturbing that for many decades there was such a degree of sniping and entrenchment of positions from therapists who should have been able to look more closely at their own responses and rivalries. It is as if diplomats had ignored their skills and knowledge and resorted in their dealings with each other to gun slinging.

The psychotherapeutic enterprise has also been an international one. There were a large number of centres of innovation, even at the beginning: Paris, Moscow, Vienna, Berlin, Zurich, London, Boston, and soon Edinburgh, Rome, New York, Chicago and California saw the development of different theories and therapeutic practice. Geographical location has added to the richness of the discipline, particularly identifying cultural and social differences, and widening the psychological debate to include, at least in some instances, sociological and political dimensions.

The question has to be asked, given the separate developments due to location, research interests, personal differences and splits between and within traditions, whether what has sometimes been called 'psycho-babble' is indeed a welter of different languages describing the same phenomena through the particular jargon and theorizing of the various psychotherapeutic schools. Or are there genuine differences, which may lead sometimes to the conclusion that one school has got it right, while another has therefore got it wrong; or that there are 'horses for courses'; or, according to the Dodo principle, that 'all shall have prizes'?

The latter part of the twentieth century saw some rapprochement between the different approaches to the theory and practice of psychotherapy (and counselling), often due to the external pressures towards organizing the profession responsibly and to the high standards demanded of it by health care, by the public and by the state. It is out of this budding rapprochement that there came the motivation for this series, in which a number of key concepts that lie at the heart of the psychotherapies can be compared and contrasted across the board. Some of the terms used in different traditions may prove to represent identical concepts; others may look similar, but in fact highlight quite different emphases, which may or may not prove useful to those who practise from a different perspective; other terms, apparently identical, may prove to mean something completely different in two or more schools of psychotherapy.

In order to carry out this project it seemed essential that as many of the psychotherapeutic traditions as possible should be represented in the authorship of the series; and to promote both this and the spirit of dialogue between traditions, it seemed also desirable that there should be two authors for each book, each one representing, where practicable, a different orientation. It was important that the series should be truly international in its approach and therefore in its authorship; and that miracle of late twentieth-century technology, the Internet, proved to be a productive means of finding authors, as well as a remarkably efficient method of communicating, in the cases of some pairs of authors, halfway across the world.

This series therefore represents, in a new millennium, an extremely exciting development, one which as series editor I have found more and more enthralling as I have eavesdropped on the drafts shuttling back and forth between authors. Here, for the first time, the reader will find all the major concepts of all the principal schools of psychotherapy and counselling (and not a few minor ones) drawn together so that they may be compared, contrasted and (it is my hope) above all used – used for the ongoing debate between orientations, but more importantly still, used for the benefit of clients and patients who are interested not at all in partisan positions, but in what works, or in what throws light upon their search for healing and understanding.

Michael Jacobs

C H A P T E R 1

Invitation and overview

An invitation

This book examines the related concepts of barriers, defences and resistance across different forms of psychotherapy. Our intention is to compare and contrast some different understandings and usages, rather than present a single model. As with other books in the 'Core Concepts' series, our main focus is on theory rather than practice, but some implications for clinical practice are discussed. Given the scope of this text and its integrative intent, we focus on areas of substantive debate and difference between therapies, rather than on detailed classification or elaboration of these concepts within any one psychotherapy. In doing this we hope to support readers in comparing some of their existing ideas about barriers, defences and resistance with alternative emphases in other therapies.

One of Freud's major contributions to psychotherapy and modern culture was the idea that there is usually more to our experience than we can notice consciously at any one moment, so that our perceptions and actions are often shaped by multiple and potentially conflictual motivations. In writing about defences and resistance, there may be areas which we have found hard to acknowledge or address directly, despite our best intentions. We invite readers to consider not just what is written here and how, but also what seems to have been omitted or suppressed as an enactment of our own resistance at play.

Similarly, in trying to make sense of the varying concepts of defence offered by psychotherapeutic theories, we suggest that readers need to reflect on their own habitual and preferred standpoints for interpretation, not merely the 'correctness' or otherwise of any given theory.

Readers are invited to adopt a critical or reflexive attitude towards their existing relationship to ideas such as 'resistance'.

This is not an easy task, however, since reader standpoints are not simply shaped by conscious knowledge and overt loyalty to a particular psychotherapeutic school or schools; they also reflect the reader's unconscious 'partial' knowledge of other therapeutic approaches which may not fit the dominant story of their avowed therapeutic model (see Sandler 1992), and so have perhaps been marginalized or suppressed in self-reflection or supervisory discussion (see Rogers 1991). Beyond these 'theoretical' influences, reader standpoints will also reflect the reader's personal history and psychosocial ecology (see Davy 2003). For example, a therapist who has been a client with an intrusive, demanding therapist may have a different attitude towards 'resistance' from other therapists who have experienced their personal therapists as nurturing and supportive, or even distant and detached. Equally, a gay therapist who is not 'out' may have different sensitivities towards themes of repression and denial around clients' sexual identity issues compared to an openly gay therapist, or to a straight therapist lacking any experiential awareness of dynamics around secret-keeping, such as excitement, shame, guilt, fear and anxiety, caution and trust.

One integrative aim for this text is to suggest ways in which divergent theoretical positions might usefully be connected. One theory may help to address 'gaps' left by another, or two apparently incompatible theoretical areas might be bridged by demystifying jargon or by identifying key ideas underlying both. However, another purpose is to highlight the pitfalls in poaching ideas and metaphors from another approach with different epistemological or ethical foundations. From the outset it is important to note that some approaches reject the use of these specific terms 'barriers', 'defences' and 'resistance', let alone treating them as 'core concepts' in therapy. Our title is therefore in some ways more congenial to the psychodynamic therapies, and so discursively helps to sustain and reinforce their historic primacy among the psychotherapies, as compared to, for example:

- Cognitive-behavioural theory, which tends to frame resistance as non-compliance with the therapist's direction and therapeutic work tasks (Beck *et al.* 1979; Dryden and Trower 1989), or as a temporary lapse in a working partnership calling for renegotiation and clarification of the therapeutic contract and the client's needs (Beck 1996; Leahy 2001).
- Solution-focused brief therapy, which understands resistance as a

conceptual error on the part of the therapist, confusing client motivation with therapist (in)flexibility (de Shazer 1984; Davy 2003).

- Personal construct therapy, which explicitly disavows defensive models of human psychology and so does not use the term 'resistance' (Kelly 1955). Personal construct therapy assumes that there is an innate human propensity to preserve personal meaning and build capacity to understand and predict the world. From this perspective, apparent resistance means that the client perceives therapy as potentially making their construct systems less viable, or as threatening to disrupt connections within the personal construct systems leading to a loss of personal meaning.

- 'Collaborative' postmodern therapies, developed out of systemic, feminist and discursive/narrative traditions (e.g. Hoffman 1993; Anderson 1997), which prefer to avoid militaristic, game-playing or oppositional metaphors for describing therapeutic processes, as part of their rejection of social structuring and interpersonal processes that are based on hierarchical power relations and competitive or patriarchal dynamics. Confusingly, in some instances of these therapies the term 'resistance' may indeed be used, but radically subverted to signal a joint endeavour by therapist and client together against extratherapeutic forces and discourses such as racism and poverty (e.g. Weingarten 1995); or as joint resistance by therapist and client against problems 'externalized' from the client, rather than seen as reflecting aspects of the client's psychological character or constitution (White and Epston 1990, Carey and Russell 2002).

We could therefore have framed the title as a question, *Core Concepts in Therapy? Barriers, Resistance and Defences*, with a range of possible answers: that is, these terms provide a starting point for debate and reflection, rather than defining the parameters of 'proper' therapy. The risk in accepting the title as it stands, even though it fits the series as a whole, is an over-privileging of those psychotherapies most at home with talk of resistance and defences. If other therapies must argue their worth in terms alien to their own value bases and epistemological foundations, they will inevitably be seen as deficient rather than different. Solution-focused therapy has no equivalent set of taxonomies for defensive processes to the psychodynamic therapies, but would flourish more readily in a salutogenic text on the 'core concepts' in therapy such as 'Connections, Alliances and Welcomings'. Conversely, it might be difficult for a post-Kleinian analyst not to judge a person-centred counsellor as hopelessly naive about the range and complexity of defensive processes and resistances in therapy.

Defining 'core concepts' within a field such as therapy can be seen in discursive terms as an attempt to fix the parameters for legitimate discussion and debate. This manifestation of power can itself be understood as a defensive process at work within psychotherapy, in the same sense that arguments for the statutory registration and regulation of psychotherapy can be interpreted as 'protectionist' manoeuvres (Mowbray 1995). The assertion of a status quo through confident terms such as 'core concepts' can be read as a defensive attempt to preserve existing practices and positions within psychotherapy against possible encroachment and challenge by other constructs ('newcomer concepts', 'surrounding concepts', 'infiltrating concepts') allied to more subjugated communities and discourses. User groups and psychotherapy survivors might well suggest a different range of core concept titles from those that tend to be used by psychotherapy professionals.

Commenting on different ways to story the history of psychoanalysis, Schafer (1992: 147) notes: 'The narratives indicate what the authors hold dear, and it is through this implementation of values that they prescribe a future.' On the one hand, the development of a 'core concepts' series suggests a certain depth and maturity to the field of therapy. On the other hand, it speaks of a defensive insecurity in the face of new resistances to the old order.

This may seem an overly philosophical digression from the 'real' material of this book. However, one of Freud's major contributions to our collective capacity for self-reflection was his insistence on the importance of attending to what is not said, cannot be said or can only be spoken of indirectly. The repression of the unthinkable and unpalatable can be traced through the lacunae and tensions amongst the spoken and legitimate. Without careful reflection on the ways in which books like this are written and read, such texts risk serving a profoundly conservative function for the psychotherapy field, reinscribing traditional ideology by inciting therapists to frame questions in well established patterns.

The structure of this book

One possible structure for a book of this kind would have been to present a series of chapters each addressing a 'recognized' psychotherapeutic paradigm (e.g. cognitive-behavioural, psychodynamic, humanistic, existential, constructivist, systemic, feminist and eclectic/integrative, as in Woolfe and Dryden 1996), using similar subheadings in each chapter to organize a summary of the key ideas. However, instead we have adopted a more discursive organization for the material which aims to illustrate axes for debate around barriers, defences and resistance, for the following reasons:

- Separate presentations of the dominant psychotherapies might help to reproduce their division rather than promote interplay and critical or dialogical exchange. The rise of integrative therapies such as cognitive-analytic therapy and interpersonal therapy, combined with recent emphases on user perspectives and evidence-based practice (e.g. Department of Health 2001; Holmes and Bateman 2002) suggests that continued organization around the interests of traditional 'schoolist' producers – e.g. trainers, supervisors and their institutions – may be unhelpful for future professional survival, let alone client well-being.

- Within a short text each 'brandname' therapy could be given only superficial coverage if treated separately. We want to avoid skimming over content which readers can already find better covered in specialized 'single model' texts (e.g. Bergman (1985) on strategic therapy, Weingarten (1995) on postmodern/feminist therapy, Leahy (2001) on cognitive therapy, Worrell (2002) on existential-phenomenological perspectives on resistance), while failing to examine connecting concepts.

- Adopting similar chapter formats to compare and contrast psycho-therapies would incorrectly presuppose that such formats and structuring are neutral and uncontested and so gloss over substantive differences within the therapeutic field. A set of subheadings derived from cognitive-behavioural approaches to therapy might form an uncomfortable straitjacket for therapeutic concepts from humanistic psychology, and vice versa.

- As an organizing theme we want to emphasize the importance of multiple contexts and perspectives for therapeutic practice. Although psychotherapeutic paradigms clearly constitute one important 'theoretical' or disciplinary context for therapy, this intersects with many others such as: differences relating to gender, class and culture; contexts concerning phases in individual and family developmental life-cycles, including the anticipation of feared and hoped-for futures; the physical/material contexts of our bodies and biology, including genetic inheritances shaped through natural selection; and the enormous range of other individual histories and contingencies which collectively constitute the selves of therapists and clients.

- We want to discuss barriers, defences and resistance in relation to the broad field of psychotherapy and its professional activities, such as supervision and training, not simply in relation to the process within a therapy session.

Overview

Chapter 2 offers some provisional, broad working definitions of barriers, defences and resistance, in order to provide a starting point for subsequent discussion. The terms are introduced in order to explore their varying meanings and contradictions, rather than as words with solid and stable meanings that we can comfortably and confidently use to describe or analyse something else. The chapter also introduces three dimensions of difference between psychotherapeutic theories and practices which affect their interpretation and use of barriers, defences and resistance. Psychotherapies may vary significantly in relation to: (a) their aims and values; (b) their ecological focus on different 'levels' of human systems, from the intrapsychic world through interpersonal processes to the social construction of meaning in extended family systems and communities; and (c) their focus on different developmental and historical/temporal phases, such as present versus future, or emphasis on individual development versus biogenetic/evolutionary influences on therapy (e.g. Gilbert and Bailey 2000).

Chapter 3 illustrates the wide variety of structures, processes and attitudes which can be understood as barriers in relation to therapy. We argue that these issues are not simply reflections of formal psychotherapeutic theories, but are also deeply perspectival, being expressions of the fit between therapists' own standpoints and beliefs and those of their clients, referrers and supervisors.

Chapter 4 discusses the varieties of risk which different psychotherapies emphasize, and how these are connected with different metaphors and mechanisms of defence.

Chapter 5 reviews the different kinds of stance or 'relationship' that therapists can adopt towards resistance, taking resistance as a specific kind of defence invoked when the therapeutic encounter itself seems to present a risk. And in the final chapter we extend the discussion of defensive concepts to the wider professional 'culture' of counselling and psychotherapy, with particular reference to issues of training, clinical supervision and evidence-based practice.

CHAPTER 2

Starting points

It is important to consider some initial working definitions of the terms that are variously used around the concept of barriers, defences and resistance, as a starting point for the more extended discussion we undertake in Chapters 3, 4 and 5. These terms need to be understood in relation to broader frameworks of language and metaphor associated with particular therapies, to highlight false similarities and differences between therapies, and to raise awareness of the differing implicit meanings of terminology used in therapy that may initially appear similar. We suggest that the more therapists can notice and reflect on these layered meanings, the more it may be possible to resolve or avoid unintended tangles binding clients (and others) closer to distress.

In presenting these provisional definitions, we also introduce three dimensions for variation across the psychotherapies, to assist comparison and interplay between the different theoretical usages. These dimensions can be characterized as: (a) aims and values; (b) a biopsychosocial or ecosystemic emphasis; and (c) the focus on particular temporal or developmental contexts for human experience.

Therapeutic metaphors, aims and values

We introduced the idea in the first chapter that the scope for integration between psychotherapies is not simply a matter of epistemological or technical compatibility, but also involves considerations of ethics and values. Terms such as barriers, defences and resistance, which at first sight appear to have similar meanings, may derive from opposed value bases or discourses, making casual eclectic approaches at best confusing and at worst actively harmful. Two psychotherapies which appear to emphasize the same level of human experience, and that initially seem highly compatible, may embody quite different purposes, such as replacing 'problematic behaviours with non-problematic behaviours which fulfil the same relationship functions' (Carr 2000: 97) in functional family therapy (Alexander and Parsons 1982), versus releasing a family's 'actualizing tendency' towards its unique potential in person-centred family therapy (Gaylin 1993).

This will be a recurrent theme in our discussion in this book, and we will argue that many barriers, defences and resistances can be fruitfully analysed in terms of difference, diversity and discrimination and in relation to our attitudes and flexibility in relation to these themes. Any given understanding and usage of these terms is connected with broader commitments and associations to certain metaphors and social discourses. These reflect the way in which the various psychotherapies emphasize different kinds of aims and values, which may range from the 'normative' restoration of functioning and symptomatic relief, through commitment to greater authenticity or clarity in experience and the maximization of human potential, to the promotion of sociopolitical resistance to oppressive dominant discourses such as heteropatriarchy.

It is insufficient simply to attend to what is denoted by a term such as 'resistance' without also reflecting on these connotations. For example, if psychotherapy is primarily understood as a kind of struggle or conflict resolution, terms like defences and resistance will take on meanings connected with fighting, warfare or political action. Reviewing the narrative theories of the psychoanalyst Schafer, McLeod quotes him on defence mechanisms as follows:

> In using the [concept] of defense, a warlike storyline is established, and in the interest of narrative consistency and coherence the [therapist] makes a commitment to follow that storyline. Such terms as abwehr, warding off, attack, infiltration, breakthrough, collapse, strengthening and rebuilding may be used: terms that have figured prominently in conventional psychoanalytic discussions of defense, and all of which may be said to be entailed and regulated by commitment to the same bellicose storyline . . . the term resistance (a close relative of defense) establishes a commitment to the same adversarial storyline.
>
> (Schafer 1992: 47)

McLeod comments:

> The point Schafer is making here is that the 'relationship is war'
> story-line implied by concepts such as 'defence' and 'resistance' is
> only one type of story that might be told about a therapeutic
> relationship. Indeed, there may be times when it would be more
> helpful to construe the same events in terms of a more 'impartial'
> or 'affirming' story-line.
>
> (McLeod 1997: 66)

Schools of psychotherapy vary in the kinds of story they like to tell
and 'perform' (Bruner 1986) about human problems, solutions and
the therapeutic encounter itself. Where psychotherapy is framed as a
joint problem-solving forum, as, for example, in cognitive and
behaviour therapies, then resistance is more likely to be interpreted in
terms of 'friction' or 'obstacles' to forward movement, or as a temporary lapse in the coordination of joint action which may lead it to be
re-termed 'non-compliance' (Beck *et al.* 1979). Therapies emphasizing
the construction of meaning and 'sense-making', such as personal
construct therapy (Kelly 1955) and constructionist psychotherapies
(e.g. McNamee and Gergen 1992; Anderson 1997) may tend to conceptualize resistance and defences in terms of misunderstandings,
poor communication, stale and impoverished story-making, or as a
therapist's unyielding attachment to a particular story line. Therapies
which emphasize the healing power of authentic relationships with
others, such as person-centred psychotherapy, or with the self-in-the-
world, such as existential psychotherapy, are more likely to
understand barriers and defences in terms of self-deception or
inauthenticity (Rogers 1961, 1989; Yalom 1980; Spinelli 2001).

This conceptual diversity is reflected in significant variations in
terminology between the psychotherapies. This is not just a matter of
one therapy using a slightly different word to stand for the same concept, in which case psychotherapy integration would require no more
than a table of similar terms or a clinician's phrase book to translate
one therapy language into another. What appears to be the same
word may stand for very different constructs and associated clinical
practices across psychotherapies.

'Non-compliance' in cognitive-behavioural therapy may indicate a
need for more detailed task-analysis and explanation of treatment
rationale, whereas the 'non-compliance' of a client viewed through a
feminist or critical psychology lens calls attention to the possible 'political' meanings being demonstrated by the client through their

non-cooperation as a form of protest. Far from being an obstacle to be removed so that the 'primary problem' can be addressed, non-compliance would be an action or communication inviting understanding, elaboration and perhaps support. Cognitive-behavioural and cognitive therapies place significant emphasis on 'doing' interventions with a client, linking these technical interventions with a specific problem formulation (Persons 1989; Bruch and Bond 1998; Tarrier and Calam 2002), and so have elaborated many responses to different forms of non-compliance with these 'doing' tasks.

By contrast, person-centred therapy emphasizes 'being with' clients – facilitating a particular kind of interpersonal climate – rather than doing to or even doing with, so that 'non-compliance' has little meaning. The Rogerian core relational conditions of congruence, empathy and unconditional positive regard are seen as not only necessary but also sufficient to enable positive change and personal growth (Rogers 1957, 1961; Lietaer 1984; compare Patterson 1984). Consequently, person-centred therapy has only a limited range of 'technical' language concerning defences, primarily concerning the construction of a 'false self' as an adaptation to conditions of worth imposed by significant others as a precondition for positive regard and forms of 'stuckness' or 'blocks' (Mearns and Thorne 1988). The defensive processes which are emphasized in person-centred theory are those which alienate a person from their own lived experience through denial or distortion, and which reshape such experience into a version consistent with the client's emerging self-concept reflecting an internalization of external conditions of worth rather than the client's organismic, authentic self (Rogers 1951, 1961). In contrast to cognitive therapy, person-centred therapy does not posit a need to interpret, explore or challenge such denials or distortions in an active manner, since the presumption is that they will dissolve naturally in the context of a therapeutic relationship which does not impose conditions of worth, as the client's fundamental 'actualizing tendency' (Rogers 1963) towards growth and well-being has space to flower and fruit.

Language and therapy

The relationships between language and psychological/therapeutic phenomena are complex. From a 'common-sense' representational perspective, words 'point towards' or represent real experiences, events and objects in the world, with 'resistance' referring to a different thing from 'counter-resistance'. By contrast, constructionist and post-structuralist philosophies of language argue that words do not straightforwardly represent the real world, but serve to create meanings and distinctions or 'punctuations' in our experience of the world. These are viewed as inherently unstable, and incomplete, but function to achieve certain pragmatic purposes in influencing or coordinating with others, so that language helps to change and order the world, rather than simply reflect it (see Rorty 1979). This is not the same as saying that the world is 'only' a matter of language, or that reality is 'languaged into being'. The point is that language has substantial effects on the material, embodied and social world – imagine being forbidden to speak your own language with your children by an occupying power. The range of distinctions we can perceive, or deem important, in the world around is also substantially shaped by the language available to us (Vygotsky 1962).

To some extent our professional vocabularies and language as psychotherapists derive from our thought processes about clients, their distress and therapy itself, but conversely our psychotherapeutic language co-determines how we understand and relate to our clinical practices and clients. If we have learnt ways to identify unconscious defences and intrapsychic processes, then we are more likely to think of our clinical encounters in these terms than a therapist whose training has privileged conscious processes, communal/interpersonal coping strategies and shared conversational exchange. As the old saying goes, to a person with only a hammer, everything is a nail. To a clinician who knows only family therapy, most problems will present as relational/family matters.

Therapists also need to consider the (mis)fit or relationship between professional vocabularies and the different languages clients use and understand. Clients and those who refer them have their own conscious and unconscious ideas about barriers, defences and resistances which they bring into the therapeutic field, as aspects of their own personal 'theories of change', i.e. beliefs about how problems and solutions are formed, and how persons can change and develop (e.g. Duncan and Miller 2000). For therapists and clients to work together requires a good-enough fit between their ways of relating and their respective theories of change. A therapist who believes that useful change requires the exploration of feelings may encounter difficulties, which could become termed 'resistance', in working with a client who believes that useful therapeutic change is most likely to come from seeking advice, brainstorming ideas and experimenting with behaviour changes between sessions.

Barriers

> For constructive personality change to occur, it is necessary that
> these conditions exist and continue over a period of time: [First],
> Two persons are in psychological contact.
>
> (Rogers 1957: 96)

When we speak of barriers, we are referring to the multiple kinds of
practices, structures and beliefs which prevent or hinder persons from
coming into meaningful psychological contact and dialogue within
psychotherapeutic settings, so that there is little or no opportunity to
develop and use a good working alliance in the first place. This could
include failures to consider therapy, problems with initial attendance
and factors promoting early 'drop-out' (Kazdin *et al.* 1997). Even if
such barriers only partially impede engagement and alliance building, there are significant detrimental implications for the process of
therapy, since there is evidence across many therapies that the establishment of a therapeutic alliance is a significant factor shaping and
predicting the outcomes of therapeutic intervention (e.g. Greenberg
and Pinsof 1986; Horvath and Greenberg 1986; Miller *et al.* 1997).

Most obviously, there may be practical obstacles operating as barriers, so denying space and time in which to meet and work together –
for example, because there is no funding – or at another level there
may seem to be no common language for communication. However,
many other factors may be involved in the construction and maintenance of barriers between people in psychotherapeutic arenas,
ranging from deficits of knowledge and skills, through personal
prejudices and preferences, to theoretical bias and organizational
dynamics such as institutional racism. Even where persons do manage to meet physically to talk, this is no guarantee that they will be
able to enter into meaningful psychological contact. The interactions
between these issues can be complex and reciprocal, such as with
theoretical prejudices and organizational culture funnelling the perception of staff training and recruitment needs, and influencing
related flows of funding.

For example, a therapist who speaks only English is not accessible
to a Deaf client using only British Sign Language, unless a suitable
interpreter is also accessible, and the therapist has relevant skills and
understanding for making use of an interpreter (Raval 1996, 2000). A
hearing therapist's unfamiliarity with using an interpreter in sessions
might seem to constitute a barrier to good psychotherapy with a deaf
signing client, reflecting a skills deficit. However, we could also ask

what attitudes and beliefs are held by the therapist, embedded within their theory of therapy, and/or within the organizational ethos, that prevent therapists, and/or their managers and trainers, from prioritizing this competency (e.g. why did the therapist choose to go on courses about working as an expert witness rather than working with interpreters?).

The term 'barrier' is less widely used in the psychotherapy literature than either 'defence' or 'resistance'. It often tends to be used in relation to organizational process and structure and the uptake of therapy services across population subgroups, rather than theorized in terms of individual therapeutic dynamics. However, like defences and resistance, barriers may manifest at many different levels, ranging from the individual through family and group systems to widespread socio-cultural practices and prejudices. As, for example, with racism, it is necessary to consider carefully the interconnections between individual, group and cultural barriers rather than complacently assume that institutional racism and the practice of individual therapists within a service are independent of one another or the broader social context.

Defences

> When the description defense is being used . . . [the subject] both knows and does not know that she sees, remembers, desires, believes, or feels something that she believes does or will involve her in some kind of dangerous situation, X. We cannot attribute a defense to her without attributing to her the knowledge (in some sense) that there is a danger to defend against. Further, not only is it assumed that the subject believes that because of X she is in danger or is about to be; it is also assumed that she believes in this threat unconsciously and that she engages in defense against it unconsciously.
>
> (Schafer 1992: 37)

Defences are processes and practices which mediate the relationship between something that seems to be both vulnerable and valued (let us call this 'V') (for example, a child's self-esteem), and something, as in Schafer's 'X', that seems to pose a potential threat to this (such as harsh criticism from parents or other significant carers). The idea of risk to something important yet vulnerable helps to differentiate defences from barriers, where it may not be evident that anything is at risk, since little contact or understanding has been possible in the first place.

However, the anticipation of an increased risk, should dialogue commence, may contribute to a resistance to dismantling barriers. For example, therapists may be (unconsciously) reluctant to engage in training about child abuse precisely because such training might make them more aware of – and potentially feel responsible for, or hurt by – extremely distressing clinical situations, which could otherwise more easily be overlooked or passed on to 'more specialist' services seen to have more expertise and resources. Similar dynamics may arise in training therapists from dominant cultural groups about cross-cultural theory and practice. A genuine commitment to learn would entail the risks of critical self-examination (but also important complementary benefits; see Mason and Sawyerr 2002), a guilty recognition of easy privilege and the recognition of injustices and much unmet need among those from less privileged groups.

Particular therapies have tended to emphasize different kinds of elements and relationships. This leads to different ideas about the types of danger to be faced, and the ranges of defences which may be invoked to deal with these. Depending on the levels at which threat 'X' and threatened 'V' are conceived, the defences which mediate their relationship may be said to operate within an individual mind between aspects of the self (as in classical early psychoanalysis, through the repression of intolerable anxieties into the unconscious mind), between persons, within families and groups (e.g. Ferreira 1963; Pollner and Wikler 1985) and/or at a collective, social scale (as, for instance, with Holocaust denial: see Harari 1995; Cohen 2001).

Schafer's psychoanalytic description constructs defences as actions or reconstructions of experience undertaken by an individual, and also invokes the central analytic construct of a dynamic unconscious. However, non-analytic therapies vary in the degree to which they accept the epistemological validity or clinical utility of the dynamic unconscious (see Spinelli 1994; Thornton 1999; see also the companion volume in this series by Edwards and Jacobs 2003) and some place more emphasis on joint actions between people and the interpersonal/communal (re)construction of meaning (i.e. social constructionism as in McNamee and Gergen 1992, and Burr 1995, rather than an individual constructivist view).

Importantly, psychotherapies also differ in terms of their preferred aims and values for the human condition. Two psychotherapies may focus on a similar level of human system (such as individual conscious experience), but value different outcomes and processes. For example, personal construct therapy focuses on the development of a flexible and elaborate set of personal constructs which enables maximal prediction and understanding of the individual's environment, whereas existential psychotherapy privileges 'authentic' experience. This means that different kinds of 'valued yet vulnerable' elements will be emphasized, with implications for the kinds of 'risk' and 'defence' that are meaningful within that therapy's terms of reference. Although self-deception or 'bad faith' (Sartre 1956) would be seen as a particular danger in existential work, this would make less sense in contemporary psychoanalytic therapy, which assumes the inevitability (and to some extent the positive functionality) of self-deception, and instead dwells more on the balance or relationships between different aspects of the mind at both conscious and unconscious levels.

Defences may also be multifunctional, serving other purposes besides the mediation of threat or danger. Evolutionary theory reminds us that biological structures and processes may come to serve multiple purposes besides, or in place of, the original adaptive function which favoured the natural selection of that biological feature (hair and skin pigmentation defend us from cold and damp or too much sun, but have also come to serve many other purposes in human society). For example, the development of an internalized working model of attachment can be understood in terms of a defensive safety strategy for a young child that is adaptive to its interpersonal environment. Minimizing demands for comfort and attention through an avoidant attachment pattern may be an important short-term survival or coping strategy for a child with a carer who is very fragile or preoccupied. However, attachment models are increasingly also being theorized as important building blocks in the development of mentalization, and affect regulation processes that endure into adult life and shape the subsequent development of other psychological processes (Schore 1994; Cassidy and Shaver 1999; Fonagy 2001).

Evolutionary theory also reminds us that, like the human appendix, sometimes organs and processes persist after the original 'reason' or circumstances which favoured their natural selection have long since disappeared. Therapists trying to understand apparent defensive processes should not assume that the risk 'X' against which the defence seemed necessary is current; it may be long gone. Clinically, this may be particularly marked in relation to work with persons who have been traumatized to such an extent that there is some dissociation of particular memories or experiences from their stream of consciousness, with these dissociated experiences seeming timeless, frozen or ever-present, rather than embedded firmly in the past within a broader context of a life that is moving on (see Freud and Breuer 1895; Dolan 1991; Loftus *et al.* 1994). Some defences may have evolved and then persisted in relation to a context where there was strong and/or prolonged anticipation of a danger to come (such as a parent leaving, or bombing by a terrorist or hostile power), even if this never 'really' materialized. Defensive processes may persist long after that which was a vulnerable 'V' has gone or has become stronger.

This implies that therapists may benefit from considering a range of temporal or developmental (e.g. individual, family/group, species) and ecosystemic contexts for defences (Boscolo and Bertrando 1993). A transgenerational history of a client's culture being repeatedly persecuted by another might have some relevance for understanding that client's family's current pattern of 'defensive' interaction with a professional 'helping' agency.

Resistance

Resistance can be understood as a specific subset of defence measures where the 'X' that seems to pose a danger for the participant(s) in therapy (or a related interaction such as supervision) is actually something about the therapeutic/supervisory process or encounter itself.

For example, it may feel unsettling for a therapist to begin to understand a client's hopes, if that client's past experience is that it has been harmful to share hopes with others (Horney 1945). Another client who has been, or still is, punched when they cry may well feel threatened by a therapist asking questions about something sad which might tempt them to tears. Similarly, if the problems brought to therapy are understood as a communication that something significant about that client's life or context needs to change (for example, that the client is being abused), then participating in a therapy which aims simply to remove the problem/symptom and restore the pre-therapy status quo may be experienced not just as unsatisfactory but as downright unsafe. If a therapist concentrates on how an adolescent client can stop cutting themselves with a razor, the process may seem powerfully resisted if the young person does not have other distress tolerance skills (Linehan 1993), or if the act of cutting serves to alarm and repel an adult trying to abuse them (Selekman 2002). These latter examples concern resistance to therapy privileging regulation and homeostasis, while the former examples may be understood as resistance to therapy which promotes change and development.

As with defences more broadly, resistances may be invoked in relation to 'past' dangers for the client, or for their family/community. A refugee client from a country where they or their friends and family were subject to surveillance, interrogation and persecution may be particularly anxious about requests to tape therapy sessions or put thoughts in writing, or perhaps feel more threatened by therapies which use many questions rather than therapies which emphasize therapist reflection and tentative statements. A client who was abused as a child because adults did not take time to listen to their distress and problems might feel revictimized by an overly rigid solution-focused therapist who only expresses interest in their strengths and interests (Dolan 1991).

These examples concern possibilities rather than certainties. Clients may perceive such echoes either as irrelevant and trivial or as helpful opportunities to experience an old dynamic in a different and better way which is reparative or transformative. Therapists who are aware of these possibilities will be more able to explore such issues with clients than therapists who have not previously considered such themes.

Although 'resistance' is a term which was more often applied to clients than to therapists in twentieth-century therapeutic discourse, similar processes may be in play for the professional, occasionally under a modified theoretical label such as 'counter-resistance' or 'co-resistance' (e.g. Schoenewolf 1993; Strean 1993). For example, a therapist who tends to be particularly distressed by childhood bullying (perhaps partly because of their own childhood experience or an unresolved difficulty with their own child's current peer group) might feel threatened by the therapeutic process if this seems to be leading towards a child client disclosing sadistic current bullying. The therapist might 'resist' by steering the conversation towards safer waters, or perhaps 'minimizing' the distress involved, or reframing the bullying as something else. Reflexive awareness of this risk by the therapist and/or their supervisor might help the therapist to tolerate and use their sensitivity to bullying as an empathic bridge for further understanding and exploration.

Resistance may relate to the therapist personally, not just to the therapeutic process, clinical approach or something transferentially evoked by the therapist from the client's past relational histories. A female client from a community which disapproves of unchaperoned contact with unrelated men may appear 'resistant' to individual therapy with a male, especially if the client's history encourages them to be deferential to professionals and the therapist does not actively support a conversation around possible choices of therapist, so that questions of gender are not explicitly raised by either. From the female client's perspective, the therapist may appear resistant if they decline a request for a chaperone in the session, or for a referral to a female colleague. It is easy to see how such mutual perceptions of 'resistance' or failure to cooperate could become self-reinforcing in a vicious circle. An alternative defence for therapists in this position is to agree too quickly to refer on, without an attempt to understand and appreciate the basis on which the client is requesting a different therapist. A male therapist may use an ethical commitment to collaborative practice combined with a gender-sensitive theoretical stance to sidestep the possibility of discovering that their client actually finds their interviewing style and manner abrasive or intrusive, rather than having a broader aversion to seeing male therapists in general.

The interpretation and management of such apparent resistances also depends on organizational values and practices. For example, the level of commitment and support for anti-racist practice in a black therapist's host agency will significantly influence the options they may feel are available in responding to a white client who asks them to be referred on to a white therapist, or to white colleagues who frequently refer their ethnic minority clients to the black therapist after initial assessment (Richards 2002). The therapeutic paradox is that clients and therapists need to feel sufficiently safe to take the risk of exploring uncertain, potentially dangerous issues (Mason 1993).

Therapeutic attitudes towards resistance

Resistances are apparently counter-productive processes which seem to hinder the ongoing therapeutic relationship and/or activity between client and therapist (or between therapist and supervisor, trainee and trainer). However, therapists can choose to adopt a range of different attitudes towards resistance, as we discuss in Chapter 5. For example, many psychodynamic therapists see resistance both as that which hinders therapy, but also as a phenomenon which potentially constitutes the most valuable focus for a transformational psychotherapy, to the extent that an absence of resistance could signal a stagnant or lazy therapy. Some approaches, such as solution-focused therapy, seem to denigrate the very concept of resistance, but also paradoxically suggest that resistance signals very important feedback from the client to the therapist about the necessary redirection for a more useful therapy (de Shazer 1984; Davy 2003). Reinterpreting resistance as attempted communication is an important stance in many therapies.

More radically, resistance hindering therapeutic engagement would not be seen as counter-productive from perspectives which are critical of the benefits of that specific therapy or indeed therapy in general. Resistance may be counter-productive in terms of having therapy sessions, but possibly beneficial for the client if having the therapy offered would have been harmful (Kitzinger 1993; Kitzinger and Perkins 1993; Masson 1993; Smail 1996), and/or would have diverted attention from other options more important for the client and their loved ones, such as medication, better housing, community support, education, employment and/or broader changes in social attitudes. Like other professional 'helping' relationships (House 2003) therapy tends to reproduce or reinforce certain kinds of power relationship or social norms and values, 'colonizing' clients with values and ideas, reflecting those dominant not only in the world of therapy but more broadly in wider society (for example, that mothers should love their children). From this perspective, often linked with the work of the French philosopher Michel Foucault, resistance in therapy can sometimes be read as attempted protest against dominant social norms and power relationships.

A biopsychosocial framework

These provisional descriptions of barriers, defences and resistance involve the idea that the psychotherapies vary in the levels of human experience they address, such as individual unconscious and conscious process, family life and cultural discourse/language. A biopsychosocial framework (Engel 1977) suggests that human experience and interactions can be analysed in terms of complex interactions between biological, psychological and social factors (Table 2.1).

At each level, a further distinction can be made between conscious, overt or explicit aspects on the one hand, as against unconscious, hidden/unaware or implicit aspects on the other. Some biological factors may be obvious to all observers, others apparent only to the individual concerned, while others may be outside awareness altogether. Cognitive therapy has tended to work primarily with individual psychological processes which are consciously and

Table 2.1 A simple biopsychosocial framework: ecosystemic levels of human experience

Meanings, processes and/or structures at the level of	*Examples*
Socio-cultural/ environmental	Cultural discourses about sexual orientation, deviance and sin. Racism. Norms and values concerning gendered roles and relationships. Economic and taxation structures. Political system, including relationship of persons to the state and vice versa. Fairy tales, mythology and cultural history. Structure of language. Physical environment and climate. The law. Spiritual/faith discourse concerning what it means to live 'a good life'.
Extended family/local community	Transgenerational patterns of belief or narratives about safety, hope and vulnerability in the context of illness and disability. Architecture of sheltered accommodation housing for a person with learning disabilities (e.g. provision or not of double versus single bedrooms, balance of private versus communal spaces, location of telephones). For a specific therapist, this level might also include identification within a psychotherapeutic school and professional discipline, and adherence to professional codes of conduct (as a form of defence for clients and professionals).
Close/immediate family (family of origin and current family)	Family of origin beliefs and stories concerning sexual relations, privacy and disability. Overt and covert messages and actions from family members about current relationships, emotional processing and communication. Family boundaries, hierarchies, subsystems and communication patterns. Patterns of conflict, closeness, distance and support. Family construct systems. Interactions with current or potential intimate / sexual partner, and their family network. For a specific therapist, this level might also include host organization or team, supervisory and other learning/supportive relationships.
Individual psychology (both conscious and otherwise)	Internalized conditions of worth, self-esteem, sense of self-efficacy. Gendered self-identity. Feelings of shame, excitement, admiration. Internalized racism,

	homophobia etc. Personal construct system. Internalized adult attachment model. Cognitive schemas. Communities of 'subselves'. Internal object-relations world. Different kinds of memory system, ranging from non-conscious and non-verbal perceptual memory through to self-reflexive autobiographical memory systems/self-narratives.
Individual skills, behaviours and procedural knowledge	Conversational skills, self-care and personal hygiene. Sexual technique and safe sex skills. Lying and flattery. Knowledge of the law and personal rights. Assertiveness skills. Self-soothing and individual emotional regulation skills.
Biological/consti-tutional factors	Temperament. Genetics and chromosomal make-up. Skin colour, sex, fertility and physical maturity. Genetic/biological factors affecting theory of mind (e.g. tuberous sclerosis), intellectual skills etc. Sensory impairment. Inherited components of behavioural control systems such as the attachment system.

verbally accessible, while psychodynamic approaches have tended to focus on individual psychological processes and structures which function outside conscious awareness. Societies are bound by both written and unwritten laws and customs, and some socially constitutive forces such as the structure of our language are extremely difficult to focus on, since they are so 'taken for granted' (Wittgenstein 1958; Billig 1999).

These 'levels' of experience constitute an important dimension for understanding and comparing different psychotherapies' ways of relating to the concepts we are examining, alongside other dimensions for variation such as therapeutic aims and values (e.g. normalization and symptomatic relief versus empowerment), and the focus of various psychotherapeutic theories on different temporal/developmental phases (e.g. past/present/future orientation).

Many concerns brought to therapy can be addressed through work at different levels. While an individually oriented therapy might help a terminally ill patient to reflect on their defences, and on adaptation and feelings concerning their own illness and mortality (e.g. Judd 1989 presents a Kleinian child case study), a family-focused approach might offer valuable complementary support enabling family members to continue meaningful and satisfying relationships in the face of serious illness and impending bereavement (Rolland 1995;

Altschuler 1997). Systemic work in other contexts such as schools may also be important (Cornish 1998). Some problems, such as child sexual abuse, require work at several different levels in order to be helpful. Individual work with children who have been abused, to understand and reclaim their experience, to find ways to think about safe and unsafe touching and so on, often makes little sense without other work to assess and enhance adult protection and care around the child, and if possible to reduce the risk of the abuser continuing to offend (Finkelhor 1984; Jenkins 1990; Bentovim 1992; Smith 1993). Strengthening the defences of the child alone may not be enough.

Sometimes a strong demand by clients or referrers for work to be undertaken at one particular level (e.g. individual work with an abused child, or family therapy for a child involved in school bully-ing) can be interpreted as a resistance to consider therapeutic change at other levels in the system (such as the parental or sibling sub-systems in their family, or leadership processes in a school troubled by entrenched bullying problems). A 'truce' may be possible in a war between a school and a family with poor relationships to one another if both can agree to scapegoat the child instead (Haley 1963).

This understanding of some resistances can be extended to insti-tutional racism in white-dominated societies that choose to structure treatment services for black people around an organizing paradigm of individual 'mental health' problems, rather than focusing resources and action on political and social anti-racist development, and fail even to recognize and document the connections between social his-tories of black minority communities and the meanings of 'mental health problems'. In one of her examples concerning African-American psychiatric survivor histories, Jackson (2002) speculates about an older black female relative's longstanding 'paranoia' about neighbours in general and white 'blue-eyed devil' people in particular as an understandable and perhaps adaptive defence against the dan-gers of living in a racist time and place in America. This particular relative managed to avoid being given a diagnosis or hospitalization, which is perhaps a sign of the effectiveness of her defence, given the vile treatment received by so many black people who were taken into the American psychiatric system.

Different psychotherapeutic models have tended to emphasize or privilege some of these biopsychosocial or ecosystemic levels more than others, and may also theorize their interactions differently. For example:

- Narrative therapy (White and Epston 1990; White 1997) has extended traditional forms of family/systemic therapy to focus more strongly on socio-cultural discourses and their connections to individual experience, but at a possible cost of losing sight of family factors (Minuchin 1998). Consequently, narrative therapy has little specific theory to help therapists to understand and respond more constructively to families who seem particularly reluctant to engage with therapy to help a young child in deep distress (Selvini-Pallazzoli *et al.* 1980; Bergman 1985). Some feminist therapists have suggested that such disregard is a useful strategic antidote to psychotherapy's history of collusion with oppressive family discourses.

- Structural family therapy (Minuchin 1974; Vetere 2001) focuses strongly on the family level, but has been critiqued both for apparent lack of interest in individual agency, sense-making and experience, and for insensitivity to normative social discourses constraining the meaning of 'healthy' family functioning.

- Cognitive-behavioural therapy directly addresses connections between individual psychology and individual skills/behaviours. Although 'conscious' modes of individual psychology were the initial focus, more recent schema-focused work (Beck and Freeman 1990; Young 1994) and Ryle's integrative cognitive-analytic therapy project (e.g. Ryle 1990, 1995) include an emphasis on unconscious processes, and also invite more connections between individual psychology and experiences in the immediate family/relational network.

- Freud's original formulations of psychodynamic approaches to therapy attempted to connect individual psychology (particularly in unconscious forms) with biological aspects of humanity, connecting a new 'science' of psychoanalysis with the evolutionary thinking cascading from Darwin. To some extent, the work of attachment-oriented therapists and evolutionary psychoanalysts (e.g. Nesse 1990; Schore 1994; Cassidy and Shaver 1999; Fonagy 2001; Fonagy *et al.* 2002) has revitalized this tradition, while also incorporating a focus on experiences within the immediate family network.

- Other analytic thinkers have moved away from appeals to biological bases, in favour of a more intense focus on an intrapsychic world of self to 'self–object' relations, linked with the study of 'two person' psychology relationships such as the early interactions of mothers and babies. Others from Ferenczi and Harry Stack Sullivan onwards have made fertile links between individual psychology and interpersonal networks of relationship, in the family, in the therapy room and within more extended groups and communities

(e.g. Horney 1945; Sullivan 1953; Ferenczi 1988; Obholzer and Roberts 1994).

Positively, these variations between therapeutic frameworks may mean that certain approaches are much better suited to particular problems than others, but may also mean that some aspects of human experience that arise from interactions between different kinds of factors are insufficiently theorized. This has implications for the manner in which therapies conceptualize defences, barriers and resistances. For example, person-centred therapy offers a useful set of understandings and approaches for attending to an individual's emotional experience at conscious and preconscious levels. However, it does not attempt to integrate understandings about affective processes derived from evolutionary psychology and brain-behaviour studies; nor does person-centred therapy attempt to problematize and deconstruct possible relationships between individuals' self-experience and wider socio-cultural and linguistic patterns, leaving the nature and value of an autonomous 'real self' uncritiqued. Person-centred conceptions of barriers, resistance and defences tend to be restricted largely to individualistic understandings, rather than family or social processes (but see Rogers 1978; Gaylin 1993).

The descriptions above are necessarily over-simplifications, since most if not all therapies would attempt to pay at least some lip-service to these different ways of constructing human experience. Nevertheless, it is a useful heuristic to have some conceptual frameworks that can be used to think about key differences and similarities between models of therapy; and to help us to remain sensitive to the dimensions of experience which any single therapeutic therapy tends to downplay or theorize rather sketchily.

Developmental and temporal perspectives on defensive concepts

A biopsychosocial framework offers a way to compare the psychotherapies in terms of their focus on different levels of the human ecology. Psychotherapies also vary in relation to their emphasis on different developmental or temporal contexts for defences. Some therapies focus strongly on the here and now. Others seek to understand the present primarily in terms of historic influences within the individual lifespan, family history, cultural change or even human evolutionary history. Others emphasize the importance of

future possibilities and developments, with the idea that we 'act into' anticipated future trajectories at least as much as we act out of past events and relationships (Penn 1985; Lang and McAdam 1997). As demagogues and rabble-rousers throughout history have known, defences may be constructed in anticipation of the kinds of future that we can conceive or are led to believe, rather than direct experience of dangers.

Although many psychotherapies acknowledge the holistic importance of interactions between past, present and future (e.g. Boscolo and Bertrando 1993), in practice there are clear differences in relative emphasis between most of them about the temporal/developmental phases they dwell on. Person-centred therapy focuses very strongly on current emotion and experience (e.g. Rogers 1951; compare Gendlin 1981), while many psychodynamic therapies may explore in more detail connections between present relationships, ideas and feelings and past experiences and events. Some body-oriented or transpersonally oriented therapies emphasize the very specific historical context of birth trauma (e.g. Rank 1929; Janov 1973; Brown and Mowbray 1994). Solution-oriented therapies tend to stress future possibilities rather than past or present difficulties (de Shazer 1988, 1994; O'Hanlon and Beadle 1997). Cognitive-behavioural therapy incorporates some ideas drawn from empiricist biology about the human evolution of emotions and cognition, threat appraisal and defence mechanisms (e.g. Gilbert 1995). Narrative therapy remains uninterested in scientific accounts of the evolutionary history of human biology, but may include some emphasis on transgenerational narratives concerning the development of individual, family and community identity, perhaps including folk psychology accounts of the original creation of the community and its people (White 2001).

Defences can be seen as a way of managing immediate threat within a current context; but within a broader temporal context some may be reinterpreted as preparations against anticipated future threats, or as strategies for achieving longer-term goals. A chess player who adopts a cramped, hypermodern opening, keeping most pieces close to the back rank, may seem to be adopting a defensive stance, but is also preparing the ground for a future counter-attack on an over-extended opponent. In an opposite sense, some current beliefs or behaviours may be understood less as defensive operations against current circumstances or feared future threats, but as misapplied remnants of old procedures which have outlived their utility. This suggests that a developmental perspective on human experience and psychotherapy is important in reviewing defensive phenomena. Understanding the perceived demands of historic contexts may help us to understand how a current defence which now seems maladaptive has been of value to a person or system (e.g. a family, community or institution) before, and may now be preserved because of distorted perceptions of current demands, or maintained 'just in case' it is needed in future.

A developmental perspective also helps to connect many defence phenomena with recurring dilemmas of change versus continuity that face individuals, families and communities over time. On the one hand, persons who cannot change also cannot adapt, and will be poorly suited both to changes in their external environment and to the inevitable changes related to physical maturation and decline. On the other hand, persons who change too readily may experience problems establishing a coherent sense of self and relating to others in predictable, socially functional ways (Linehan 1993). At a family or communal level, groups which cannot (or are forbidden to) hold on to traditions, life-stories and culture risk dissolution and extinction (Fredericks 2003).

Viewed through a developmental lens, defensive processes can often be understood as attempts to regulate and slow the pace of change and development (Mahoney 1991), which may be thoroughly adaptive in some measure but cause problems if development becomes arrested, or is diverted down pathways which are unlikely to fit well with current and future demands.

Conclusion

This chapter has offered some initial working definitions of barriers, defences and resistance, noting that these terms entail varying connotations within different kinds of therapeutic discourse, which partly reflects the use of different metaphors, such as growth, conflict and understanding/prediction. 'Barrier' usually refers to difficulties in making and maintaining contact so that psychotherapeutic work might then take place, while 'defence' involves the attempt to eliminate or reduce some perceived threat to something valued but vulnerable. 'Resistance' can be understood as a particular subclass of defensive processes, when there is something about the therapeutic process or encounter itself which seems to constitute a danger.

We have also presented three dimensions of variation across the psychotherapies as conceptual aids to integration, comparison and interplay of these concepts: (a) biopsychosocial or ecosystemic levels of human system; (b) temporal or developmental contexts; and (c) the aims and values in psychotherapy. In the light of these starting points, over the next three chapters we expand the possible understandings of the main terms of our title.

C H A P T E R   **3**

Barriers

Necessary conditions for therapy

It is generally thought that before therapy can begin, three minimal conditions must be in place. First, there must be a perceived problem or challenge. Someone, usually the client, must believe that this might be resolved by a person or persons entering into therapy. Some therapies with values oriented towards personal growth or development, such as person-centred, personal construct and transpersonal therapies, emphasize the challenges of movement towards more optimal functioning or a 'higher level' of development (e.g. Kelly 1955; Rogers 1961; Wilber 1980; compare Anderson 2001), rather than assuming that the client is dealing with a problem as such. Growth orientations frame therapy as an opportunity or developmental process rather than a need.

Second, the person who identifies a problem or challenge must be one of those persons who have therapy, or alternatively must be able to compel or persuade other people to come for therapy: for example, when courts use multisystemic therapy programmes (Henggeler 1999) as an alternative to custodial sentencing for young offenders.

Of course, mandating attendance is not the same as enabling therapy. Therapists may then be faced with one or both of two challenges: (a) finding effective ways to invite the attending client to engage with a therapeutic process, e.g. through 'motivational interviewing' (Miller and Rollnick 1991) and/or (b) managing their relationship with the mandating referrer consistently with the therapist's ethics. A school counsellor who is asked by a headteacher to 'counsel' an unwilling adolescent in order to change their behaviour might be able to negotiate some shared agenda of value to the adolescent (e.g. 'ways to get the headteacher off my back'), but might also or instead need to question or refuse the referral (for example, if the headteacher is asking the counsellor to prevent an adolescent from developing a gay or lesbian identity).

Third, there needs to be someone willing and able to take on the role of therapist to the identified client(s). In the example above, a school counsellor ethically committed to equality for gay, lesbian, bisexual and transgendered people in society might refuse to accept the mandated referral, and offer consultation to the headteacher instead of the adolescent. It follows also that therapists may sometimes experience themselves as 'mandated' to do work which contravenes their own values in the context of an 'invitation they can't refuse'. This is likely to have a significant effect in the dynamics of 'resistance' in therapy. The broader point shared with clients is that 'willingness' to work in therapy is not a simple all-or-nothing matter, and is highly dependent on wider contexts and discourse intersecting with the personal values and commitments of those involved.

One way of thinking about barriers initially is as phenomena which are in some way 'external' to therapist and client that hinder a service provider and service user from meeting and talking together in the first place. For example, a city-based psychotherapy department serving a rural area may find that attendance by people without a car is substantially lower than for car-owning clients from higher socioeconomic groups. The location of the psychotherapy clinic and a lack of good public transport could be viewed as barriers between the therapists and certain clients which are not directly attributable to psychological characteristics of therapist or client.

Barriers can also relate to inflexible attitudes, unresolved personal issues, mismatched expectations and skill deficits. For example, equitable client access to a city-based psychotherapy service for a rural population might be enhanced if the therapy team was willing to work more flexibly through greater use of outreach services, telephone consultation and so on, and had the resources to put such changes into practice. As Macpherson's (1999) inquiry into the racist murder of Stephen Lawrence powerfully reminds us, discrimination can pervade 'helping' systems in many guises, ranging from overt, intentional discrimination by an individual through to barely visible, unintentional discrimination permeating the practices of an organization as a whole.

Echoing psychotherapy's traditional preference for middle-class and articulate clients, some therapists may not wish to work with people from 'lower' socio-economic groups, or with clients with chaotic lives who find it harder to coordinate with clinic-based appointment systems. Others may resist change to a contained working life in a well ordered clinic, preferring not to spend time travelling to clients' homes and communities, or working the more unsociable hours that a more community-oriented service might entail. Status issues may also be involved, with senior staff less subject to pressures to change working patterns, so that flexible outreach services become staffed primarily by less experienced clinicians. These issues may be more or less consciously recognized by the therapists concerned.

A professional's own psychological make-up and therapeutic issues may contribute to these dynamics. For example, therapists with insecure attachment histories might have a greater need for a secure clinic 'base' from which to work than a securely attached therapist (Holmes 2001). If therapists do not experience good enough containment and holding from their host organization in forms such as effective management, reliable and empathic supervision etc., they might cling more tightly to the institution as a secure base, and offer greater resistance to service reconfiguration. However, these 'psychological' factors will exist in some balance with 'real world' constraints and priorities for these clinicians. Even the most securely attached, confident clinician may reasonably be reluctant to work unsocial hours because of the inconvenience to the rest of their life, such as relations with friends and family. Such commitments may constitute very 'genuine' barriers to flexible engagement in therapy for therapist or client, while also offering scope for rationalizing resistance to change in the therapeutic process.

Clients' limited knowledge about therapeutic services or therapists, or significant prior misunderstandings about the therapies on offer, are also likely to constitute factors which may compromise the development of a therapeutic alliance at an early stage (e.g. Holmes and Urie 1975; Plunkett 1984). This suggests that therapists should actively provide accessible and relevant information about their services so that clients can make informed choices. However, this assumes that it is clients who need to change rather than therapists. If a certain group of clients tend to believe that therapy involves advice-giving, this can be framed as a 'misunderstanding' by a service offering a non-directive therapy. Although this barrier of misunderstanding can then be addressed by educating the clients about non-directive therapy, an alternative approach is to learn more about the clients' current knowledge and expectations, and tailor the therapeutic service to fit this better: for example, by offering more directive or psycho-educational work.

The issue is not simply a choice between focusing on the knowledge of clients or of therapists, but concerns power differentials. The therapist has greater definitional power within the therapeutic frame than the client, and chooses whether to educate/socialize the client into their model, or to adapt their approach to fit the client better. Pilgrim (1997) cites Bannister on this theme as follows:

> Clearly the relationship between therapist and client is initially neither reciprocal nor equal. If you are the therapist then you and the client are on either side of your desk, in your office, on your patch. Your presence signifies qualifications, expertise and prestige; the client's presence signifies that he or she has 'given in', 'confessed failure'. You, as therapist, represent (socially if not in fact) the healthy ordered life while the client represents 'sickness' and confusion. You prescribe the pattern of the relationship . . . You may decide to be non-directive, but, even so, it will be you that decided to be non-directive. You may negotiate all things but you do so from a position of power.
>
> (Bannister 1983: 139)

Some asymmetries of power in therapy are probably unavoidable dilemmas demanding ongoing management and reflection, rather than problems which can readily be solved for good. However, including current and potential users in planning and prioritizing the development of new therapy services may help to make the work of dismantling barriers to therapy a joint endeavour, rather than something which the client has to do, albeit with some assistance from the therapist. Red Horse (1997) discusses how a therapy programme to address alcohol misuse was negotiated with a Native American community. The therapists adopted an explicitly collaborative approach, aiming to share decision-making with the community elders. Instead of promoting one approach with the 'best external evidence', they met with the elders to explain the theoretical assumptions underpinning several models, including psychodynamic and humanistic therapy, so that the community could select an approach which seemed appropriate for their community as well as the problem. The elders disliked psychodynamic ideas, preferring humanistic models as more compatible with their values, although they were puzzled that Maslow's (1968) hierarchy of needs was inverted; they saw spiritual development as a person's most basic need.

Poor knowledge may be a factor for the therapist: for example, if the therapist lacks an understanding of respectful and acceptable ways to engage a client from a particular cultural community, or if the therapist holds theoretical prejudices about the non-viability of therapy with certain populations. Freud's view that older people were not suitable for psychoanalysis is still echoed today in continuing ignorance among many psychotherapists about the scope for constructive work with older adults, particularly where there are cognitive 'impairments' such as those caused by the dementias (see Kitwood 1997 for alternative ways of conceptualizing such changes). This professional prejudice can be further compounded by others, such as scepticism about psychotherapies with clients who have significant learning difficulties and/or limited verbal skills.

A therapist's skills are not simply accomplishments, but also expressions of their values in action. Therapists who work with young children without prioritizing the use of developmentally appropriate communication methods, such as modified language, play, stories and songs, pictures and other non-verbal means (e.g. Wilson 1998), are demonstrating a lack of commitment to Article 3 of the UN Convention on the Rights of the Child, that 'children should be informed, consulted and involved in any matter affecting them, according to their age and understanding', by failing to provide the communicative scaffolding which would help the child to participate meaningfully.

More subtly, barriers may make it hard for persons to have any meaningful conversation around an agenda for therapy even when they do meet. For example, a client may feel unable to share their reasons for wanting therapy in terms that the therapist can understand because of cultural differences which the therapist neglects, such as implicit and explicit expectations about permissible topics of conversation between men and women. This barrier would be further reinforced if the therapist lacked language, theoretical concepts and supportive professional contexts, such as good supervision, to reflect on gendered aspects of selves and relationships (Down *et al.* 2000) or on other socio-cultural variations (Falicov 1995).

Conflicts of interest, and connections between barriers and defences

Distinctions between barriers and defences are not as clear cut as even our chapter divisions suggest. Apparent barriers may arise where the nature of the client's concern is in some way overwhelming or incomprehensible for the therapist, or where the client simultaneously both wants and fears understanding. As a rough heuristic, barriers most accurately refer primarily to situations where there is some deficit in structures, skills or understanding which prevents therapist and client from trying to establish a good connection. By contrast, defences and resistance relate to situations where experiences and feelings can, at least in principle, be shared and jointly explored together, but where available resources, skills and understandings are not fully used because of a perception (accurate or distorted) of some risk or threat from such reflection. Defences and resistance concern the capacity to tolerate and process such experiences jointly and the degree of agreement about common aims in the work together.

Further complexity arises, since some powerful defences against potentially distressing threats may include 'failing' to notice these in the first place through partial or complete denial, highly selective reinterpretation or minimization. A heterosexual therapist's lack of knowledge or understanding of social and sexual relationships in the gay communities may constitute a barrier to effective work with a gay client, even to the extent of preventing a client from disclosing, or the therapist from realizing, the client's sexual orientation. Frosh (1997: 191), commenting positively on Freud's capacity to recognize some of his analytic failings in hindsight, writes:

> Psychoanalysis has been engaged with homosexuality from its inception, with Freud struggling manfully against the recognition of lesbianism in his 'Dora' case. His famous footnote added at the end of the case history is an explicit recognition of a blind spot that continued to trouble the vision of psychoanalysis for generations afterwards: 'The longer the interval of time that separates me from the end of this analysis, the more probably it seems to me that the fault in my technique lay in this omission: I failed to discover in time and to inform the patient that her homosexual (gynaecophilic) love for Frau K. was the strongest unconscious current in her mental life . . .' (Freud 1905b: 162).

If the therapist is reflective about their own sexual identity, and has a broadly positive attitude towards social diversity, then education through training, reading, supervision and perhaps some charitable risk-taking by the client may enable the therapist to start dismantling this barrier (McCann *et al.* 2000). However, this may not be possible if the therapist feels deeply uncomfortable about reflecting on his or her own sexuality and engaging with difference. In such instances, the barrier can better be understood as a defence for the therapist, maintained through their inaction.

Similarly, if a client in the example of the rural psychotherapy service mentioned above attends appointments only intermittently, citing transport problems as the reason, some therapists would wonder about more psychological reasons for non-attendance. This might concern resistance to the therapeutic work in progress, or a perceived need to defend an aspect of the client's experience, which might otherwise be in danger if they attended too readily. For example, the client might fear that their regular supportive contact with a local GP will be reduced once they are seen as 'fully engaged' by the psychotherapy team.

The presence of a client, a therapist and some kind of problem or challenge is clearly not a sufficient condition for useful therapy, simply a necessary precursor. If an individual client is forced to come to therapy, while utterly disagreeing that there is any problem to be resolved, the potential for therapeutic interaction of any kind is severely limited, perhaps simply to problem-solve how to persuade the coercive referrer to back off (Cox 1974; Berman and Segal 1982; Pilgrim 1988). Even where someone has identified a 'need' for therapy, there may simultaneously be contrary factors or conflicting interests which will interfere with the referral process. The identified client may be in 'two minds' about whether to come or not. Therapists too may have mixed feelings about the prospect of encountering a new client, or referrers may themselves be conflicted. Such conflict may be conscious and apparently rational – for example, relating to the resource implications of referring for therapy – but it can also relate to less obvious factors. For example, if a staff member in a residential care home for adults with dementia allows herself to 'notice' the personal distress of a resident or relative that might be addressed through therapy, this might seem to open the floodgates for the staff member not only to notice the referral needs of other residents/relatives, but also to experience more fully the pain and sadness of her own working context. Routinizing work and treating patients as objects of care rather than suffering fellow beings are common defences in professional caring (Menzies-Lyth 1960; compare Freud and Breuer 1895: 232, re Elizabeth von R.'s nursing of her father and other family members).

The interrelationships between institutional 'barriers' and the 'defences' of the constituent members may be particularly complex, as, for example, when the heterosexist ethos of a training institution is produced by, and also in turn helps to reproduce and validate, the heterosexist attitudes (and/or internalized homophobia) and practices of individual therapists (Cunningham 1991; Frosh 1997). Institutional culture and expectations can construct or reinforce barriers. Therapists working in a service which uses a framework of scheduled appointments and 'efficient' utilization of scarce clinician time may experience an organizational resistance to flexible engagement and contracting with clients who have very chaotic and unpredictable lives, or who come from cultural groups which tend to view time as a plentiful rather than scarce resource (Levine and Bartlett 1984; Shiang *et al.* 1998; Owusu-Bempah 2002).

Therapy may be barred when a therapist is required by their employer, or by the local clinical culture ('the way we usually do assessments around here is . . .'), to focus on particular concerns or issues, whether diagnostic or otherwise, which do not intersect with a client's motivation for talking with a therapist. For example, if a therapist in an inpatient eating disorder unit feels required to encourage a client with very low body mass index to eat more, at a time when that client is preoccupied with their appearance to others or with overwhelming feelings of shame and hate, then the quality of the therapeutic alliance may be compromised for a while (with a lack of common purpose between client and therapist easily reconstrued as the client resisting 'proper treatment'). Even if therapy did proceed in those circumstances, there would still be some barriers in place within the sessions, constraining permissible themes for exploration and understanding. It is meaningful to think of barriers to particular therapeutic themes and processes, not just barriers to therapy as a whole. Similar dynamics may occur for services trying to engage with clients who make dangerous attempts to harm themselves, or with families who may be harming their child.

The main point here is not that risk assessment is necessarily an unhelpful barrier to therapy, but rather that there may be higher contexts (other kinds of action and understanding) which need to be privileged over the context of therapy at least for a time. The presence of serious ongoing child abuse in a family demands that adults privilege action to ensure child protection even if this constitutes a barrier to therapy. Sometimes it is possible simultaneously to coordinate protective and therapeutic agendas (for example, if a therapist and client can work to understand connections between anorexic eating patterns and self-hate and their effects on the client's life), but this is not always the case. However, the way in which protective action is taken may have implications for barriers in future therapy. If an assessing therapist fails to explain the limits of confidentiality appropriately to children or other family members, who then disclose child abuse which makes the therapist break confidence, a barrier of distrust and expectations of betrayal may be established for the child and family and taken forward into future therapeutic encounters: 'This man is a therapist. The last time I told another therapist something really important, they broke their promises to me' (Jenkins 1997; compare Bollas and Sundelson 1995).

Diagnosis, labelling and barriers

Therapists working in public service contexts with a strong culture of 'treating' mental illness may feel constrained to interview within an 'assessment–treatment' model which prioritizes early comprehensive information gathering above the establishment of relationship and trust, and the negotiation of possibilities and preferences consistent with the client's wishes and the agency remit (Griffiths 2003). Where the biomedical tradition is deeply rooted, this dynamic may be further reinforced by pressure to fit clients within treatment frames centred on diagnostic categories rather than individualized formulations or understandings. This may be particularly the case where diagnostic categories have become associated with (semi)standardized 'evidence-based' treatment protocols and so seem to hold out a prospect of more 'efficient' treatment from a purchaser's perspective (Tarrier and Calam 2002). Therapeutic agencies need to balance psychotherapeutic fidelity and flexibility for each individual client with equity and access for all potential service users. We are not suggesting that medical/psychiatric diagnosis is necessarily incompatible with sensitive psychotherapeutic engagement and constructive therapeutic process and outcome. The point is that foregrounding early diagnostic clarity over engagement introduces some risk of compromising therapeutic process, although it may convey other benefits.

Diagnoses themselves, and labels more broadly, may have mixed effects as barriers to therapy or in overcoming barriers. Certain diagnoses in mental health settings have historically operated to exclude some patients from talking treatments. Mental health patients diagnosed as showing a psychosis tend to be offered primarily drug treatments rather than psychotherapy (Karen and Bos 1981; Pilgrim 1992). Borderline personality disorder (BPD) in particular has often been criticized as a diagnosis barring the labelled person from access to meaningful psychotherapeutic treatment by negatively prejudging the person's likely response to psychotherapeutic interventions.

Kutchins and Kirk (1999: 177) go further in suggesting that a BPD diagnosis can also operate as a defence for professionals 'to undermine the credibility of women who complain about their male psychotherapists, with that diagnosis depriving vulnerable patients of the defence against abuse which professional complaints procedures should provide'. However, these issues are contested and changing, as new therapies are developed which claim to address psychosis and BPD more effectively (e.g. Linehan 1993; Young 1994; Ryle 1997). These labels may then become a means to overcome barriers and gaps in existing service provision: for example, by securing home-visiting or out-of-hours services, or therapeutic packages which can alternate flexibly between intensive support and longer-term supportive therapies, sidestepping frustrating 'revolving door' re-referrals.

Some diagnoses offer 'entry tickets' to psychotherapies, which might not otherwise be provided (perhaps most obviously demonstrated when courts ask for psychiatric reports before sentencing). Adults seeing a GP in primary care may be offered only brief counselling at the practice with little choice of therapist or therapy, unless the GP can be persuaded that the patient has a significant psychiatric disorder requiring onward referral to secondary specialist mental health services. Many parents fight hard to acquire diagnostic labels for their distressed children in order to access specialist resources (such as attention deficit/hyperactivity disorder clinics) which might not otherwise be available, although at times such battles for labels can also be read as struggles to avoid more comprehensive psychosocial assessments (e.g. Law 1998; Bennett 2003): for example, to conceal coercive family processes.

An enduring tension is the degree to which accepting the award of a professional diagnosis might remove barriers to some therapies, but at the same time set up a barrier between the client and aspects of their own experience, which are not encompassed within the expert understanding of a diagnosis. If a client comes to believe that they have a certain label, then they may feel constrained to offer the therapist ideas and experiences which fit within this professionally defined frame, rather than allow themselves to share experiences and 'local knowledge' (Geertz 1983) which are at variance with, or marginal to, their diagnosis. Similar dilemmas can confront a therapist working under the banner of a specialist clinic, who might feel that the work context and expectations regarding their professional expertise imposes constraints to pursuing other understandings. We are not arguing that diagnosis or certain labels are necessarily unhelpful, rather that unhelpful barriers may arise if people come to be understood too narrowly or 'thinly described' (Geertz 1973) through the context of their diagnosis to the exclusion of the other contexts shaping their expression of their lives.

Differential access to therapy

Some questions around diagnoses and labels are instances of a broader class of barrier, concerning differential access to psychotherapy and counselling. Therapies may be restricted to certain kinds of problem, and specific groups of the population may have different levels of access to therapy for similar kinds of problem.

At the beginning of this chapter we stated that one minimal precondition for therapy is that there must be a perceived problem or challenge. Humanistic theories conceptualize this more broadly than many other models, with an understanding of therapy as enabling personal growth and maximizing human potential (Bugental 1967; McLeod 1996), rather than treating pathology or resolving a problem *per se*. Transpersonal therapies take this even further, typically by proposing that ordinarily conceived mortal limits on 'optimal functioning' can be transcended through progression into higher, transhuman/ transpersonal levels of being and experience (Wilber 1980). However, funding barriers may reflect mismatches between the aims and values of particular psychotherapies and the potential arenas for their practice. Contemporary Western public health care tends to understand therapy relatively narrowly, in relation to dysfunction and pathology rather than to optimal function. Hence, there will be substantial funding barriers preventing access to such modes of humanistic and transpersonal therapy, unless they attempt to recast themselves as adjunctive interventions to support the resolution of some illness problem (and so risk compromising their main therapeutic aims).

Although this suggests that public health care prejudices about suitability for therapy might constitute a barrier towards the provision of humanistic and transpersonal therapies, from a service provider's perspective such decisions might be an important means of preserving limited resources for access by those in society who are most needy or vulnerable. Barriers to psychotherapy sometimes operate as differential access to different forms of psychotherapy, rather than absolute barriers to any kind of therapy. Is it right and proper that poorer, less articulate and less powerful members of society have only limited access to forms of therapy which are more open-ended or long term? Alternatively, is it right and proper to use scarce communal resources to fund therapies which do not seem directly to address significant and immediate individual suffering?

Certain population subgroups may also be excluded from therapy through lack of skills and specific competencies (language, interpreter use etc.) on the part of the professionals. A particularly obvious form of restriction is the greater ability of those in higher socio-economic classes to pay for therapy in private practice. Waiting lists in the public sector represent a kind of barrier to psychotherapy through rationing, which money can circumvent. Particular modes of therapy, such as telephone counselling, time-limited sessions or group therapy formats, may help to eke out limited therapeutic resources, but in so doing construct differential barriers to particular forms of therapy.

Referrers differentially recommend and refer clients for particular forms of therapy depending on their beliefs about the fit between a particular client, the apparent problem and the kind of therapy. Some of these beliefs might be well founded, but others can reflect prejudice against particular social groups, and so reproduce discriminatory practices by creating differential barriers to service access. For example, some referrers might hold a belief that people with learning disabilities are not suitable for therapies which involve attention to talking, thinking and reflection, and so fail to refer for therapy altogether, or tend to refer to therapies with strong behavioural and directive components. Kitwood (1997: 98) has described similar prejudices concerning the use of talking therapies for people with dementia, against which he argues that:

> There are some respects in which they may be more open than others to therapeutic change. For example, they are often extremely sincere and open in expressing what they are feeling and needing, whereas many people who are cognitively intact hide behind conventional masks and pretences. People who have dementia are markedly sociable, whereas our culture often engenders withdrawal or self-isolation. Psychotherapy generally aims to help a person lower their psychological defences, and in a sense become more vulnerable; many people who have dementia are in that state already, even though it was not of their own choosing.

This is not an argument that all forms of therapy are equally well suited to all persons or problems. However, differential referral rates for therapy of any sort, and for different forms of therapy, are often not clearly linked to an obvious and uncontested evidence base.

Sometimes, the very absence of an evidence base may itself constitute a barrier to a particular therapy, if this narrows the range of therapeutic options available to a referrer (we discuss this further in Chapter 6). Certain population subgroups are more likely to be pressured into some forms of therapy, rather than held at bay. Two glaring examples are the enforced psychiatric treatment of political detainees in the Soviet Union (Bloch and Reddaway 1977) and the coerced treatment of gay, lesbian and bisexual orientations as psychopathological (Kutchins and Kirk 1999) throughout much of the twentieth century. Pressure on others to enter therapy can sometimes be understood as a form of defensive process on the part of individuals or larger groups.

Clients and/or referrers may be unwilling to work with particular models of therapy, or indeed with particular therapists or organizational contexts. For example, if therapists working with alcohol users insist that clients must remain 'dry' while entering treatment, many potential clients will be excluded. Similarly, some clients may insist on seeing therapists of a particular sex, sexual orientation, ethnicity, age etc. If these demands cannot be met, or the therapist/provider is unwilling to accommodate such demands, this constitutes an obvious barrier to therapy. Some barriers of this kind can usefully be understood as boundaries, helpfully dividing up territory for different uses. However, many of these issues relate to potentially contentious value positions, rather than universally agreed protocols for therapy. How should a public health provider respond to clients who will only see a therapist of the same ethnicity, and how would this relate to social power differentials? If a white adult client in the UK protests against referral to a black therapist, should this be treated any differently from a gay adolescent male asking to see a gay therapist, or a Muslim woman asking to see only a female Muslim therapist?

Conclusion

In this chapter we have explored issues and conditions which may form barriers towards establishing a meaningful therapeutic encounter. These factors may range from cultural constraints and mismatches, through organizational processes and structures, to the attitudes, skills and knowledge of therapists and clients. We have suggested that barriers may be partial or selective rather than all-or-nothing, and may apply more to some client groups than others, or hinder work on some therapeutic themes more than others. We have emphasized the importance of recognizing potentially conflicting interests in the therapeutic encounter, and reflecting on the issues of choice and values which underpin these.

Different therapies offer different theoretical tools and skills for noticing, understanding and addressing barriers at varying biopsychosocial levels. Within the same clinic a systemic therapist and a psychoanalytic therapist are likely to focus on different barriers towards service user access, although there may be good scope for combining these insights within a biopsychosocial framework. There may also be variations between therapies at the level of method or technique in terms of responding to barriers (so, for example, scheduling flexible one-off 'drop-in' sessions to accommodate clients who say they find it hard to attend regularly will have different therapeutic implications for a solution-focused practitioner, a psychodynamic therapist and a person-centred counsellor). These considerations will intersect with individual therapists' capacities to apply their theoretical models creatively and flexibly in practice. Overall, however, the concept of barriers is probably less controversial across the psychotherapies than those of defences and resistance, as we discuss in the next two chapters.

CHAPTER 4

Defences

Defining defences

The concept of defences is probably more widely recognized in some therapies than barriers, although there is a clear link, as we suggest below. In our attempt to approach this concept as broadly as possible, we might say that the term 'defence' implies at least three elements that are closely related:

1 It suggests something vulnerable which is also important, desirable or valuable, which may be at risk.
2 It implies that there is something that seems to pose a threat, constituting a potential risk or attack.
3 A defence is something that can mitigate or remove the apparent risk by mediating the relationship between the first two elements.

These elements may variously be persons or 'parts' of persons; they may be families or organizations; they may be beliefs held by an individual or by a group; or they may be patterns of individual or collective behaviour. Particular therapies have tended to emphasize different kinds of elements and relationships, ranging from the intense focus on aspects of the individual self in object-relations psychodynamic theory, through to a focus on patterns of language and behaviour between individuals and sections of the community as described by contemporary narrative and discursively oriented therapists.

The perceptions of risk and vulnerability which defences mediate may or may not be accurate, and may vary across contexts, over time and depending on the standpoints from which they are evaluated.

Defences may also vary considerably in how useful they are and what 'side-effects' they have, both in the short and the longer term. Defending against strong emotions by an emphasis on dispassionate rationality may be a functional strategy for a professional involved in child care proceedings, because this may aid good decision-making, but if 'over-activated' it could also hinder appropriate empathy with the hopes and fears at stake. As we discuss below, insecure attachment patterns can be understood as defences against problematic patterns of caregiving, which may have some short-term adaptive/survival value for an infant, but may contribute to enduring patterns of relationships and emotional management that can be impoverishing for some people in later life.

Sometimes, attempted defences against certain kinds of threat may not only be ineffective, but actually add to the problem pattern. For example, citing Newth and Rachman (2001), Tarrier and Calam from a cognitive-behavioural viewpoint write:

> In patients suffering obsessional-compulsive disorder it has been suggested that concealment from others of catastrophic fears is an additional manifestation of avoidance and neutralizing behaviour characteristic of this disorder. Concealment, resulting primarily from a fear of the negative reaction of others, serves to sustain the obsession by preventing exposure to alternative interpretations of the significance of the thought.
> (Tarrier and Calam 2002: 322–3; compare Salkovskis 1985)

This can apply at different levels of human system besides the individual. Whole families may defend through the social construction of a family 'unreality' (Pollner and Wikler 1985), against, for example, the traumatic realization that they are being affected by intrafamilial sexual abuse, managing to 'pretend' to themselves and to the outside world that it is not happening. This local culture of denial, dissociation or minimization then further contributes to a context in which further abuse can occur without disclosure, acknowledgment, restitution or healing. In Bentovim's terms (1992), the family becomes a trauma-organized system, from damage resulting from abuse but also through counter-productive attempts to defend against the pain of trauma.

Barriers as defences/defences as barriers

To continue a theme from the previous chapter, it can be difficult to distinguish between a barrier and a defence, since aspects of both are sometimes present. Maintaining barriers can sometimes be understood as a defensive process against some perceived risk, while many defensive processes become rationalized as unavoidable barriers. A therapist's fear of making home visits to try to engage highly distressed and chaotic clients can easily become translated into a sensible need to make efficient use of scarce clinic resources by minimizing travel time. The organizational barrier of resource constraint is harnessed to defend against the therapist's anxiety.

Writing about the tendency of many family therapists to avoid or downplay direct work with children, Wilson (1998) argues that many therapists lack confidence, skills and fluency in work with children, but explain these away through rationalization, such as the greater effectiveness of work with parents alone, or a desire to protect children from hearing about distressing family situations, or a fear that children might disrupt the session by misbehaving or needing the toilet. Wilson suggests that this helps 'therapists to avoid taking the risk of staying with the difficulties presented and working with children despite the pain or the "messiness". Zilbach (1986) found that some therapists' experiences of their own childhoods were so painful that they found it difficult to enter into the serious world of children's play because such playfulness was discouraged in their own upbringing' (Wilson 1998: 10). Rationalization can be an important shared defensive process for both therapists and clients, as, for example, where a family therapist lacking confidence in their skills with children colludes in absenting children with parents who wish to conceal a distressing situation from their children.

What are the functions of defence?

What do defences protect, and from what? Early classical psychoanalysis presented the active repression of unacceptable or frightening aspects of self out of consciousness as the principal engine of psychic life, to the extent that repression created and maintained the realm of the unconscious (Billig 1999; Jacobs 2003). Initially Freud placed a strong emphasis specifically on the repression of instinctual sexual desires and ideas (Eros), but from the 1920s he developed his dual-instinct theory, which acknowledged what he felt to be the equal power of aggressive and destructive urges (the death instinct, Thanatos: Freud 1920) in an ongoing conflictual counterbalance with sexual, generative and expansive wishes. Freud believed that what was repressed always tended to return ('the return of the repressed', e.g. Freud and Breuer 1895; Freud 1910, 1915), leading to a constantly shifting dynamic balance between unconscious but powerfully charged material and a veritable armoury of psychic mechanisms operating both to maintain repression and to minimize the dangers of leaks into consciousness that nevertheless inevitably occurred: for example, by converting an unacceptable thought or impulse into a joke (Freud 1905c; compare Billig 2002); or more pathologically by attributing a particularly toxic feeling or thought to another 'self' as in multiple personality disorder (Braun 1986), or to external agents inserting or broadcasting material into one's mind from outside of the self's control, as in some psychoses (Freud 1911).

Repression was theorized as the primary defence in psychoanalysis, in which dangerous thoughts and/or feelings were kept from consciousness ('primary repression'), with a range of secondary defences to respond to the tendency of this repressed material to seep or burst back into conscious awareness ('repression proper': see Erdelyi (1990) for a review of Freud's shifting uses of the term 'repression'). In some of Freud's early writings these dangerous thoughts and feelings are seen as stemming from risks and traumas in the embodied and interpersonal real world, in particular from frightening or confusing sexual experiences involving other people. However, Freud came to reject the hypothesis of seduction as a *universal* explanation for hysteria (initially through a letter to his friend Fliess in 1897 (Masson 1985b), later presented more publicly in Freud's *Three Essays on the Theory of Sexuality* (1905d)), and placed a greater emphasis on the origins of unacceptable ideas and emotions in intrapsychic fantasy, rather than actual childhood, family or social experience. Mainstream psychoanalysis became less concerned with distress arising from what had actually happened in people's lives, and more focused on distress arising from unease or imbalance between aspects of the self.

As part of his critique of psychoanalysis, Masson describes this shift as a major betrayal of the experience of Freud's patients. In his *The Assault on Truth: Freud's Suppression of the Seduction Theory* (1985a), Masson suggests that this theoretical shift in psychoanalysis can itself be understood as a defence against the pain which therapists can face in clinical practice. However, Jacobs argues that Masson overstates this case, misrepresenting Freud as retreating completely from the idea that psychological problems result from sexual abuse. In fact, Freud continued to acknowledge that 'seduction' (sexual abuse or incest) was *sometimes* a key factor, but no longer believed this was always the case (Jacobs 2003: 111–14).

This tension between interpreting psychological experience in terms of intrapsychic processes and interpersonal experience is very active today across the therapies, and even within individual models of therapy. For example, Tarrier and Calam (2002) note that modern cognitive-behavioural therapy is pulled between a flourishing cognitive emphasis on intrapsychic process and (mis)interpretation of experience, and an older and initially more 'radical' tradition of focusing on behaviour and actual interaction in an embodied physical and social world.

Freud's own primary emphasis was on the actual psychic life or 'material' which became repressed or at least deeply disguised or distorted. By contrast, his daughter Anna Freud initiated and presided over an explosion of interest in the multitudinous mechanisms of defence as a primary source of therapeutic focus, shifting the emphasis on to the structures and patterning of mental life rather than the specific urges being defended against (e.g. A. Freud 1936).

A person who has committed an act contrary to their 'usual' standards of moral behaviour may have very self-critical thoughts and feelings. They might 'defend against' these self-accusations by offering rationalizations about unusual mitigating circumstances for the act, by trying to forget about the act in question, by downplaying the consequences and significance of the error or perhaps by blaming someone else for 'making' them commit the act. It can be exceptionally difficult for some abusers to recall, reflect on and explain their own abusive actions (so that abusive events become 'deleted' from memory as though they had never been, or consequence minimized, or responsibility distorted and denied), partly through fear of external sanctions and consequences, but partly through a need to defend the abuser's self against the unbearable self-knowledge of their horrendous actions (e.g. Rogers 1989; Bentovim 1992; Smith 1993).

Similarly, some persons who have been abused may find it difficult to understand and acknowledge any pleasurable sensate experiences or relational rewards associated with their abuse, and manage this through wholesale repression of the experience, not simply to protect themselves from memories of suffering, fear and humiliation, but also to protect themselves from confusing feelings of guilt, responsibility and ambivalence towards their abuse. Children in particular may be prone to this, since they lack the vocabulary and world experience to make sense of an abusive episode in the context of normal physiological/bodily functions, and to distinguish caring relationships that legitimately involve physical contact from physically expressed sexuality (Ferenczi 1932).

Billig (1999) goes further, suggesting in his discursive reanalysis of Freud's 'Little Hans' case (Freud 1905a) that young children may actually be trained and inducted by those around them into forms of language and mentalization which actively preclude the capacity to think or ask about certain themes (for example, through adult implicit modelling of quick self-correction, self-punishment or self-distraction when such themes are hinted at), rather than children simply 'lacking' language or concepts for certain experiences. Billig's point is that the developing child's inner speech and mental landscape reflect an internalization of the conversational and relational possibilities demonstrated interpersonally in the young child's social world (Fonagy *et al.* 2002). In learning to speak we also learn what we should not say, so that language is simultaneously both expressive and repressive in its overall form and function. This implies that children may sometimes find it hard to speak of abuse not because they lack the skills and understanding to do, but because they have been taught, and incited to use, the skills and knowledge needed to conceal or defend abusive practices. (This should not be read as blaming children for hiding abuse. Instead, Billig's ideas can be used to highlight the pervasive subtleties of grooming, which can entangle children in their own oppression as part of the abuser's defence system.)

The relationship between 'internal' and 'external' threats is complex. Young children thwarted by a parent may experience murderous rage towards the adult for preventing the gratification of their desire, yet simultaneously 'know' at some level that it is vital for their existence to maintain a positive relationship with their carer, and hence struggle to inhibit the full expression of their rage. The evolutionary psychoanalyst Nesse (1990) has argued that one of the most reliable ways for a social and communicative animal like a human to hide something from another member of the same species is to hide it away from one's own consciousness.

However, the significance of the relationship between what is to be protected, the defence and the potential risk clearly also depends on the contexts in which these elements are embedded. There are different things at stake in a friendly argument involving personal insults between two lovers and in a dispute between candidates at a political hustings, although of course the 'friendly' context of a lovers' argument may transform into a hostile one if boundaries are overstepped inadvertently, or if the cumulative implicative effect of many arguments begins to change the definition of the relationship from a loving context to a failing one (Cronen and Pearce 1985). Some problems encountered in psychotherapy may concern problematically distorted

perceptions of risk fuelled by idiosyncratic and self-defeating contextual interpretations: for example, when it may seem too dangerous
to leave a violent partner because of a strong belief in one's
own incompetence and vulnerability in the wider world (or from
an object relations perspective, the risk of being in an unsafe relationship may be perceived as less than the risk of not being in a relationship at all).

'Mature' defences and coping strategies

A distinction is sometimes drawn between immature and mature
defences, particularly in therapies strongly influenced by psychodynamic theory. Defences such as splitting, denial and projection are
seen as developmentally 'primitive', while others such as suppression,
altruism, sublimation, anticipation and humour are often regarded as
more 'mature' achievements which are built on other linguistic, cultural and interpersonal competencies acquired through developmental socialization processes (Vaillant 1992).

However, even with therapies which focus strongly on defences,
mature defences are not necessarily be seen as superior to primitive
ones. Primitive defences may be highly adaptive and appropriate in
certain circumstances. The definition of a 'mature' defence depends
on the standards and expectations of the community passing judgement in relation to the task or situation in question. The humour of
soldiers on battlefields and staff in some hospital wards (Menzies-Lyth
1960) may weave disconcertingly from apparently adaptive ways of
managing highly distressing situations, through to a disconcerting
denial or distortion of the suffering of other persons, even to an
extent that is dehumanizing. Similar dilemmas regarding the use of
humour may be seen in supervision and training sessions with
therapists who work in clinical contexts which provoke high anxiety
and frustration: for example, with people who repeatedly harm
themselves.

There are considerable overlaps between the construct of defences
in therapy and the idea of 'coping strategies' found in the literature
on health psychology: 'To constitute coping, strategies should aim at
lowering the probability of harm resulting from the stressful
encounter and/or reducing emotional reactions. Whether or not
these strategies are successful in reaching the goal of managing the
stressful situation is not part of the definition of coping' (Stroebe and
Stroebe 1995: 202).

In psychotherapeutic discourse, the term 'defence' is often reserved for ways of coping with threats which are unconscious or otherwise 'out of ordinary awareness'. This may be understood in a variety of ways: for example, in terms of deeper, hidden or 'automatic' (perhaps pre-verbal) mental processes as in psychodynamic, constructivist and cognitive approaches; or in terms of highly selective self-attention and divided experience in existential therapy and person-centred psychotherapy; or in some systemic/family therapies in terms of operation as an emergent property arising from patterns of activity and thought between persons, which are not the result of an explicit agreed plan; or in terms of discursive/linguistic processes not located within individuals but 'speaking through' persons, as in narrative and postmodern systemic/critical therapies and Lacanian psychoanalysis (Billig 1999).

By contrast, many, though not all, 'coping strategies' are readily accessible to conscious reflection and planning. Principal coping strategies identified by health psychologists (e.g. Folkman *et al.* 1986) include:

- confrontive coping, e.g. 'I tried to get the person responsible to change his or her mind';
- distancing, e.g. 'I didn't let it get to me, I refused to think about it too much';
- self-controlling, e.g. 'I tried to keep my feelings from interfering with other things too much';
- seeking social support, e.g. 'I talked to someone who could do something concrete about the problem';
- accepting responsibility, e.g. 'I realized I brought the problem on myself';
- escape-avoidance, e.g. 'I tried to make myself feel better by eating, drinking, smoking, drugs etc.';
- planful problem-solving, e.g. 'I knew what had to be done, so I doubled my efforts to make things work';
- positive reappraisal, e.g. 'I found new faith'.

Much health psychology focuses on coping in relation to external stressors around the person (such as adaptation to a new group living situation after an independent life), or to stressful physical encounters impinging on the person directly (e.g. an impending operation or worsening disability). Psychotherapeutic concepts of defence range more broadly, including not only these physical/ environmental stressors, but also defences to internal emotional or psychological dangers and pressures, such as one's own feelings, self-evaluation, beliefs and conscience, as well as interpersonal (relational) sources of anxiety.

Descriptions of coping strategies in the health literature tend to resemble the 'mature' defences of psychotherapy rather than primitive ones. This may help to underline that mature defences are not necessarily effective or positive ones. Coping with a persistent bowel pain by 'distancing', as described above, is similar to the defence of suppression, but may turn out to be fatal if the pain stems from an undiagnosed bowel tumour in an early stage of growth. 'Accepting responsibility' for being raped ('I was so stupid, I shouldn't have drunk so much and flirted with them') would, we hope, be seen by most therapists as a misplaced and counter-productive defence against pain and distress (tantamount to denial), accepting responsibility inappropriately through a kind of identification with the oppressor, and through turning against the self, which might even result in further harm through the internalization of a persecutory 'object' or hostile self-belief.

Complexity and chronicity

Defences vary considerably in complexity and chronicity, ranging from highly transient and relatively isolated actions and processes (such as blaming a single misdemeanour on someone else to escape punishment and/or a personal sense of guilt), through to enduring patterns of feeling, thinking and behaving dominating most areas of lived experience (such as the severe and chronically disabling dissociative experiences of persons with multiple personality disorder, or the chronically ingrained patterns of avoidance shown by adults who have lived with obsessive-compulsive disorder for many years without treatment). The purported extent of the elaboration and chronicity of defences is sometimes reflected in terminological distinctions between 'defence mechanisms', 'security operations' (Sullivan 1953), 'non-compliance' and 'blocks', as against language implying more enduring and pervasive phenomena, such as defensive complexes and positions (such as Klein's paranoid-schizoid defence against persecutory anxieties produced by the death instinct Thanatos: Segal 1964), defensive strategies, personality traits, 'false self' (e.g. Winnicott 1965) or 'self-system' (Sullivan 1953), character armour (Reich 1945), deep/core schemata (Young 1994), core constructs (Kelly 1955; Fransella 1989, 1993) and family scripts (Byng-Hall 1995).

At one extreme, defences may be theorized as transient responses to specific threats, with effects limited to well bounded aspects of mental or social life. Many of the classic psychoanalytic defence mechanisms identified by Anna Freud (1936) can be understood as discrete mental operations in this way. At the other extreme, a defence may consist of a complex and enduring pattern of beliefs and behaviours with pervasive effects, to the degree that it virtually becomes a strategy for living (which may or may not be adaptive in the long run). From a cognitive perspective Borkovec *et al.* (1990) have suggested that intense worrying can block access to *other* specific feared images and thoughts (perhaps particularly those associated with trauma: Brewin 1997) but can become habitual and pervasive, producing generalized anxiety disorder. Several psychotherapeutic theories which rest on the notion of a 'true' or authentic self suggest that an entirely 'false self' may be constructed as a long-term defensive response to a problematic social and psychological environment. Writing about Winnicott's ideas, Jacobs comments: 'Normal development, even where it runs relatively smoothly, inevitably involves the development of different defences . . . The false self is a natural part of development, built up on a basis of compliance . . . a defensive function, which is the protection of the true self' (Jacobs 1995: 58).

The idea of a defensive 'false' self has less relevance to therapies which do not assume an 'essential' self of some kind (for the concept of the self, see the companion volume in this series by Brinich and Shelley 2002). While person-centred therapy aims to exorcise a 'false self' which acts as a barrier between the organismic 'real' self and an individual's self-perception, constructionist and constructivist therapies alike presume the existence of multiple forms of self called forth in different interpersonal contexts (Mair 1989, Shotter and Gergen 1989, Harré 1998). Different versions of self may be experienced as creating more or less possibility for developing positive relationships and meaning, but are not seen as more or less 'real' in any absolute sense. However, it might still make sense within constructionist and constructivist therapies to think in terms of constraints on possible forms of living, which have been imposed by defensive necessities. Threats and dangers may mean that an individual has only been able to develop or express a relatively impoverished range of identity positions, which may not fully reflect the richness of their lived experience or value and commitments (Jenkins 1990; White and Epston 1990).

Attachment styles and working modes are examples of complex and enduring patterns with defensive functions (Fonagy 2001; Holmes

2001). Insecure attachment patterns can be understood as adaptive but defensive strategies for coping with particular parenting styles and capabilities, which may in time become templates for managing more diverse relationships as internalized attachment models (Main *et al.* 1985). Recently, there has been growing interest in the possibilities of attachment theory as a vehicle for linking family functioning, interpersonal behaviour, intrapsychic representations and evolutionary biology (Cassidy and Shaver 1999; Sloman *et al.* 2002), while Schore's work (1994) on developmental infant neurobiology attempts to synthesize the biological with individual and dyadic psychoanalytic perspectives. He argues that the relational and emotional scaffolding provided for early infant mentalization and affect regulation has profound consequences for the development of the child's brain, with enduring influences on subsequent cognitive-affective capabilities and self-organization/self-structure (Fonagy and Target 1997; Fonagy *et al.* 2002).

Even disorganized attachment can be understood as an attempted solipsistic defence against unsustainable emotion through vigorously pulling in/pushing away from affect-arousing relationships. However, this occurs in ways which are very hard for others to predict and coordinate with, so that disorganized attachment constitutes dysfunctional emotional regulation, inasmuch as it precludes the possibility of enlisting others to help to manage emotions, and to help the distressed person to learn and internalize new ways to regulate affect. Human beings are social animals, and emotional expression and regulation is a social accomplishment and communal responsibility. Persons with disorganized attachment styles are at risk of shouldering the whole burden alone, as it is hard for them and others to connect in a relational and emotional ecology (Hill *et al.* 2003). This makes sense in the context of an early environment in which it felt too dangerous to stay connected with others for any significant length of time, or where it was dangerous to allow others to predict and understand one very well. From a therapist's perspective, this means that the disorganized attachment style of some clients may pose a substantial barrier, particularly if the therapist's training or agency setting does not provide them with a flexible repertoire of styles, places and pacing for engagement.

Many therapies see highly pervasive and disablingly extreme defensive processes as associated with severe, developmentally early threats, such as severe neglect or abuse in early infancy. A substantial body of developmental research supports this in relation to disorganized attachment (Cassidy and Shaver 1999; Fonagy *et al.* 2002).

However, different pathways and factors contributing towards pervasive and disabling defences are suggested by other therapies, including:

1 'Run-away' feedback loops, in which small defensive patterns become deeply ingrained and amplified through vicious circles or faulty reality-checking procedures (Ryle 1990), even where the initial threat was limited (Watzlawick *et al.* 1974).
2 Chronic but highly unpredictable stressors.
3 Responses to bewilderingly different or invalidating current contexts in comparison to previous experience: for example, where a refugee client has made an enforced, unplanned major migration across cultures under traumatic circumstances into an uncomprehending and invalidating new host community.
4 Struggles with experiences which are deeply taboo within the dominant cultural discourses.
5 Responses to severe existential threats such as terminal illness or the anticipated death of one's child.

Although individual therapies vary in their emphases on such pathways, from an integrative perspective it is important to consider the possible interactions and multiple contributions from such patterns towards the development and elaboration of severely disabling, counter-productive defensive processes. An individual who has needed to develop a dense network of defensive processes to survive and tolerate early abusive experiences may be doubly at risk after an enforced migration to an alien culture, particularly as the previous defences may not work outside the context in which they evolved.

Developmental and evolutionary perspectives on defences

Commenting on the complex social history of human language, the philosopher Wittgenstein (1958: 8e) writes: 'Our language can be seen as an ancient city: a maze of little streets and squares, of old and new houses, and of houses with additions from various periods; and this surrounded by a multitude of new boroughs with straight regular streets and uniform houses'. His suggestion is that our present-day language contains many tangles and ambiguities which reflect past origins and usages as much as present needs, and that sometimes we become confused or misled if we too easily take language for granted. From a developmental perspective, some of our propensities for relationship and interaction (including defences) are similarly like an ancient city, progressively constructed and reconstructed through the incorporation of new features into existing structures and patterns, and the reclamation of old materials and strategies to serve new purposes reflecting contemporary challenges.

Schools of psychotherapy differ in their preferred developmental frameworks (see the companion volume in this series by Simanowitz and Pearce 2003), and hence in their depiction of defensive tasks and problems which may face individuals and families over time. Some forms of brief therapy (Cade and O'Hanlon 1993) disavow interest in developmental perspectives. Some other models such as cognitive-behavioural therapy incorporate developmental perspectives relatively loosely, as 'contextual' information rather than as foreground. Some therapies such as person-centred counselling emphasize developmental processes within an individual lifespan. Others such as the systemic therapies attend to transgenerational patterns including intergenerational patterns for perceiving and defending against threats and attacks. In recent years, theorists in evolutionary psychology and psychiatry have begun to interpret psychological, cognitive and emotional processes in the context of species survival and reproduction across many generations, in that natural selection operates to favour specific genetically informed structures and processes (e.g. Gilbert 1995, 1998).

Social constructionist and transcultural therapies (e.g. McNamee and Gergen 1992; Waldegrave 1990; Weingarten 1995; Anderson 2001) stress the need to understand patterns of individual or family experience, including defence mechanisms and strategies, in relation to the wider experiences and histories of particular socio-cultural groups.

> There are three related assumptions of social constructionism that are relevant. First, the terms by which we understand the world are a product of historically situated interchange between people, not reflections of an objective reality outside of us that can be known through ever more accurate empirical investigations. Second, the degree to which a given understanding prevails is not fundamentally dependent on its objective validity, but on its use by a community of speakers, listeners, writers and readers. Third, what we know and understand is shared with others and these negotiated meanings influence the actions we can take.
>
> (Weingarten 1995: 1–2; referring to Gergen 1991)

For example, men and women may tend to use different forms of defence to address similar threats, not just because of their individual histories but also because the cultural histories of men and women are different, and the cost/implication of using any particular defence (such as aggression against an attacker, or withdrawal from an abusive relationship) may be different for a man and a woman. The way in which something is experienced or anticipated as a threat will also be culturally mediated. The anxieties, emotional dilemmas and excitements associated with adolescent sexual maturation may have different ramifications for heterosexual as against gay/lesbian young persons within communities where heterosexuality is the norm, varying also with any given community's history of celebrating or tolerating or persecuting minorities.

A contemporary defensive process or structure may have been formed through the modification of older features, and may continue to serve other longstanding/prior functions besides the defensive one. This may or may not be adaptive. In other cases, something which began as a defensive process (such as the use of humour to deflect playground hostility) may have been recruited, or sublimated (Freud 1930), to serve another primary purpose (such as becoming a professional comedian), leaving the defensive function as residual or normally dormant, except perhaps in times of particular stress (when it might become difficult to adopt a sufficiently 'serious' or emotionally involved attitude to relationship or lifestyle problems outside the work context, such as children's distress after the death of a family member).

Processes may be developmentally old, in the sense of deriving from an earlier phase of an individual's lifespan development, or phylogenetically old, in evolutionary terms, as something originating among pre-human ancestors and continuing in adapted form in *Homo sapiens*. Contemporary therapists are usually more familiar with the former style of understanding the influence of the past on the present, but in recent years advances in evolutionary psychology and psychiatry have offered more holistic ways to understand the mind–body interaction, which steer away from reductivist dichotomies between psychosocial and biobehavioural explanations (e.g. Gilbert and Bailey 2000; Sloman *et al.* 2002).

It seems likely that vomiting had an early adaptive biological function, in helping to rid the body of noxious substances rapidly before they can do serious damage. Although this function remains, some persons with eating difficulties seem to have co-opted vomiting to serve other purposes, some of which may be psychologically defensive interpersonally (for example, to keep others away, or to keep some others involved), or intrapsychically, as an attempt to rid the self of unacceptable feelings and images, or to ward off feared future personal developments (such as a sexually mature self, through the suppression of physical sexual characteristics).

Gilbert (e.g. 1992; see also Gilbert and Allan 1998) has suggested that aspects of clinical depression can be understood in terms of an excessive or 'runaway' process aimed at defending resources, particularly in the context of failing struggles for group status or social rank. From an evolutionary standpoint, it is adaptive for an animal to compete successfully with others for valuable but limited resources such as food, shelter, parental care and potential mates. Faced with both an opportunity and potential competitors, it is advantageous for animals to be able to express dominance and power to claim the resource. However, it is also an adaptive advantage (at both individual and group selection level) to be able to short-circuit the competition process to achieve a differential allocation of resources, without excessively destructive competition between individual members. Many symptoms of human depression (fatigue, social withdrawal, flattening of expressed affect, apathy) seem well adapted for interrupting conflicts between the depressed individuals and those around them. In social terms, they signal defeat and withdrawal, and invite the renegotiation of group roles and relationships.

There are some obvious parallels here to older formulations in other psychotherapy literature. For example, from an existential-phenomenological perspective Laing suggested that states of depression and psychotic withdrawal could be understood as attempts to heal and grow through an intense introspection, facilitated by withdrawal from the everyday social world (Laing 1967). This emphasis on self-healing influenced Laing to pioneer therapeutic communities as sanctuaries within which persons could find and heal themselves, while being protected from external dangers and distractions. This is a vision of therapy akin to McLeod's anthropologically informed presentation of psychotherapy as the provision of a 'liminal space' (a culturally sanctioned borderland outside ordinary social experience) to enable a transition from one phase of life to another (McLeod 1999; compare Turner 1969).

In contrast to Laing, contemporary evolutionary psychology does not attempt to recast depression as a desirable or romantic experience. Although severe clinical depression may have some roots in interpersonal processes which have had adaptive significance in human evolution, that is not the same as saying that any given episode of depression is necessarily positive. Clearly, severe depression can and does have very maladaptive consequences for the depressed individual and those dear to them, up to and including death by suicide or self-neglect. Gilbert's emphasis is more on depression as an 'overshoot' or pathological exaggeration of a biologically innate tendency to withdraw quickly in the face of probable defeat or loss of social status and rank. Depression can be viewed as a marked, potentially dysfunctional, manifestation of a wider interpersonal defensive strategy, which is sometimes very adaptive.

This evolutionary perspective highlights the potential value of trying to understand the possible meanings of problems such as depressive symptoms. The problem for which a client comes to therapy may be an important defence against something else that is possibly more perilous. If a therapist simply focuses on lifting or interrupting a client's depression, without understanding something of the contexts which produced this and which the client inhabits, there might be a risk of returning a client to a risky situation with fewer defences.

Confusion versus conflict

Some of the differences in the psychotherapies lie between models emphasizing confusion-based explanations of human distress (misunderstandings, distorted cognitions and attributions, skewed belief systems etc.) and those which highlight conflict-based explanations (such as the attempted repression of unacceptable ideas and feelings, or managing intolerable choices between different kinds of basic need, such as affection versus safety).

However, conflict and confusion may overlap in complex ways. For instance, the perception of risk and the activation of a defence may arise from confused misinterpretation of oneself and of those around one. It is common in child and adolescent mental health services for children to believe they have been brought to therapy for punishment, or at least to be 'told off', and an early task in engaging children is to explore the fears and hopes associated with the consultation (Wilson 1998). Of course, this may include assessing how much some carers actually do expect the therapist to be punitive or support them in being so, and self-monitoring how punitive the therapist may become if faced with a 'difficult' child or obnoxious behaviour.

Some forms of confusion may operate as defensive processes. Some men in privileged patriarchal positions are unable to bring themselves to understand why feminists 'make such a fuss' about gender inequalities. Paedophiles who misinterpret children's responses to abuse as favourable can protect themselves in this way from guilt and self-punishment. This defensive function then contributes in aspects of therapeutic work with offenders to the great difficulty in, but also clinical necessity of, focusing on accepting responsibility for abuse and appreciating its impact on survivors.

Perceptions of risk vary according to the perspective from which they are assessed, and one person's confusion or misunderstanding may be understood by their interlocutor as a conflict or risky situation. A therapist may believe that an impasse has developed in therapy because of a simple misunderstanding about the nature of a homework task, while a client with a personal history of domination and exploitation by others may become frightened about a therapist's attempt to control them, or invade their life outside the therapy hour by prescribing homework.

Lemma (1996) notes that therapists working with psychotic clients need to consider very carefully how much interpretative or interactive work to undertake, since invitations to make sense of personal experience may themselves be experienced as profoundly threatening or destabilizing rather than a relief of mental pain (Steiner 1994); and also because some delusional beliefs adaptively seem to offer personal relief and comfort regarding historic losses and setbacks rather than distress (Roberts 1991). Lemma comments that this perception of therapeutic risk can itself become a defence for the therapist who may be wrestling with 'the most frequent but unconscious anxiety [which] is the fear of being driven mad by the patient' (Rosenfeld 1987: 18), so that 'it remains incumbent on us to question any reluctance to engage in interpretative work with the psychotic individual. By remaining purely supportive in our role, we may be expressing our own unconscious need to inhibit in advance the person's aggressiveness towards us or our unconscious fear of facing the psychotic parts of our personality' (Lemma 1996: 176–7).

However, also based on a discussion of Rosenfeld's work and Frosh's (1991) analysis of psychosis, Parker *et al.* write:

> We might interpret the discourse and practice of psychopathology as a 'psychotic defence'. We want to argue here that the images of madness that are relayed in clinical texts construct a reality for the clinician that is fantastic and frightening, and that it is then no surprise that psychiatrists who write and read this stuff should be so frightened of being in the presence of someone who is 'mad'. This type of talk, and the practice that

follows from it makes it difficult for practitioners to work across the divide between reason and unreason. The demonology of psychotic experience in psychiatric texts increases the gap, and makes all the more 'other' the experience of those it talks about.

(Parker *et al.* 1995: 116)

Defences as multifunctional: the example of projective identification

A recurrent theme within this text concerns the possible multiplicity of functions served by any psychosocial process or construct including apparent defences. An important example of a defensive process that is (potentially at least) multifunctional is the phenomenon of projective identification in psychotherapy. A therapist may find himself or herself experiencing strong emotions in a session, or perhaps when reviewing a case with his or her supervisor, with no clear apparent cause. Projective identification refers to the idea that such feelings can sometimes be understood as belonging to, or originating from, the client, rather than being grounded in the therapist's own lived experience and ongoing emotional dilemmas. Put very crudely, therapists may find themselves experiencing their client's sense of shame, for instance, as though it were their own.

In psychoanalytic theory, projection was originally conceptualized by Freud (Freud and Breuer 1895) as a form of infantile defence against an emotion that is intolerable to the ego, put out into the external world, analogous to excreting an indigestible toxic waste product. Melanie Klein (1946) elaborated this into the idea of projective identification, in which different parts of the self might be split off and projected into the outer world not simply to dispose of them, but as a means towards a reassuring sense of control over the other who can be 'compelled' to have a certain experience.

These Freudian and initial Kleinian understandings both clearly describe defensive processes attempting to reduce the threat resulting from certain kinds of internal feelings and ideas. However, Bion and later Kleinian theorists suggest that projective mechanisms do not simply serve defensive purposes, but also function as communication initiatives between the person who projects and those adults who are available to receive the projection (Mitchell and Black 1995).

Bion believed that projective identification was not just an omnipotent phantasy of splitting off parts of the personality and depositing them into another, but that the infant is also trying to make his reality bearable by causing it to be experienced and understood by this mother. The mother's function as a processor of unbearable feelings is known as containment.

(Garland 2001: 181)

In turn, the mother (or another 'processor', such as an attuned therapist) may communicate back a transformed understanding of that which was originally projected. In Bion's complex terminology, the recipient of the projections may be able to transform 'primitive beta elements' into 'alpha elements' of mental life which the infant can more readily experience and integrate (Bion 1977). This depends on the 'processor' having sufficient psychological resources to process the initial affective state, and to soothe both themself and the infant. This enables the baby (or client) to achieve a different relationship to their own original experience, and in time come to internalize some templates for organizing and processing affective states. The client may project into the therapist some powerful experience, which is hard for them to assimilate or comprehend. Given sufficient capacity, the therapist may then be able to help the client to develop a richer understanding of what they had initially experienced. In this interpretation, anxious feelings are projected not because they are 'toxic' and need to be permanently evacuated to remove a danger, but because there may be value in helping others around the person projecting to understand what it feels like to be that person. This creates possibilities for influencing the behaviour and caregiving of these others. In turn, these others may be able to help the originator of the projected feelings to develop more understanding of what these feelings signify and how to contain and manage them more autonomously.

An interactional understanding of projective identification suggests not only a communicative function, but also a developmental function. The mother/therapist provides scaffolding (Vygotsky 1962, 1978) for the infant/client to experience something which would otherwise be some way out of their reach, with the developmental possibility that this interpersonal scaffolding process may become internalized as an elaboration of the infant/client's own mentalizing capacity. This is consistent with an idea of people as social beings, who evolve their sense of self through reciprocal interaction with others. We come to know who and what we are through our relationships with others and through their feedback to us about how they experience us (e.g. Sampson 1993).

Summarizing, the idea of projective identification in psycho-therapy has evolved through stages of conceptualizing it as: (a) a defence through excretion/expulsion; (b) a defence through attempted distancing and control; (c) a communication of affective state and experience; and (d) a part of an interactional developmental process, enabling communication but also enhancement and maturation of processes organizing experience and affect. (For further discussion of projection and projective identification, see the companion volume in this series: Grant and Crawley 2002.)

The clinical significance of this discussion is to highlight the strategic choices available to the therapist in noticing and responding to experiences of apparent projective identification. Holmes and Bateman (1995) suggest that projective identification is both defensive and communicative, and that it is the kind of sensitivity and response offered back by the therapist which will determine whether the defensive or communicative function is most prominent. If the therapist responds to the client's projection as though they have been attacked, then the client may construe their ongoing relationship with the therapist as a hostile or adversarial one, and activate more defences. Conversely, if the therapist is able to respond constructively and empathically to the projective communication then the client may feel less isolated and better supported, and more able to lower or suspend some defences which are in place.

For example, a therapist may be working with a client who is trying to describe a sexual assault. In the course of the session, the therapist might come to experience a wave of distaste bordering on contempt or even disgust that makes it hard for them to remain in empathic connection with the client's account. The therapist could see this as an aberration unconnected with the client's account, attempt to dismiss these feelings and try to reorient towards the session (in effect, the therapist attempts to defend against their own apparent weakness or failing). Alternatively, the therapist could see this wave of revulsion as a displaced emotion from the client that they would rather be rid of and are trying to dump on the therapist. This might orient the therapist towards the attempted provision of a cathartic experience, or towards an empathic reflection on the intensity of the client's distress.

However, the therapist might also understand their experience as an attempt by the client at defensive control, perhaps pushing the therapist to keep his or her distance or to reproduce a predictable and familiar role of punishing or criticizing the client, for the therapist's weakness or failings in being assaulted. This might orient the therapist towards curiosity about how important others have reacted towards the assault on the client and to other distressing times in the client's life. Into what position is the client trying to put the therapist, and how could this be understood? (McDougall 1986 suggests a theatrical metaphor for the consulting room, as a stage for transferential re-enactments of past dramas; compare Klein 1952.)

Alternatively, the therapist could choose to understand such projective identification less in terms of defence, and more in terms of communication. It is an expression of the request for help in processing an important but incomprehensible or indigestible experience; perhaps the client is also feeling confused and overwhelmed by feelings of self-disgust. This would invite a therapeutic posture oriented towards joint meaning-making and exploration around the projected emotions in order to differentiate and recontextualize them. This may be, for example, in relation to broader discourses concerning violence, sex, gendered responsibility, shame and vulnerability, and/or in relation to other events in the client's personal history, such as earlier abuse, that could then be more easily reassimilated with other aspects of the client's identity.

There are parallels between these different understandings of projective identification and related therapeutic postures, with different interpretations and responses that clinicians can adopt towards resistance (see Chapter 5).

Therapeutic aims in relation to defences

Most psychotherapies accept that defences of some kind can be very appropriate and helpful, and regard with great suspicion therapists who see their primary task as dismantling a client's defences. Therapists' interests in defences often concern the balance between adaptive defences that are well integrated with other kinds of personal processes and aims, and those defences which are either (a) effective against a particular current risk but at too high a price in other respects or (b) fighting non-existent or negligible dangers, perhaps relating to historic risks which have long since passed. An example of (a) is an inner-city victim of a violent street assault who defends himself against future attacks by remaining isolated in his bedroom for years on end; and an example of (b) is a child who starts to refuse school so as to avoid contact with dog faeces, for fear of contracting a fatal illness, after a bout of food poisoning which made the whole family sick.

Defences may be adaptive or functional in some respects (such as maintaining short-term physical safety in an abusive relationship by remaining very quiet and acquiescent); but may simultaneously be maladaptive or constraining in other ways, to an extent that significantly impairs personal development or social functioning (for example, making it very difficult to re-evaluate the worth of the relationship, or explore strategies for changing or leaving the abusive relationship). Defensive systems can be regarded as aiming to assist survival by creatively rearranging sources of conflict and risk (Vaillant 1992), but with varying degrees of effectiveness and future implications.

Sometimes therapy may involve reducing overactive and/or maladaptive 'stuck' defences, or reappraisal of the risks defended against, while at other times therapy may involve focusing on the development and elaboration of a greater range of more adaptive defences. Therapy might also involve making more appropriate and effective use of existing defences, as, for instance, in supportive psychotherapy (van Marle and Holmes 2002). Therefore, different therapies might involve:

1 Developing a more adaptive or flexible set of defensive stances to address some continuing risks or fear (coping and preparation, problem-solving, reorganization of personal resources).
2 Placing current risks in proportion or in clearer perspective, revising outdated or inaccurate patterns and perceptions (reappraisal, reality-checking, insight, 'good faith', organismic valuing, expanding and performing meaning).
3 Focusing on the development or release of actions, ideas and relationships which are not directly related to the apparent risks but which may have been neglected or 'frozen' by the efforts involved in defending against some danger (restoration, rebalancing, holistic development, solution-development).

Therapy may involve a combination of these emphases, but particular psychotherapeutic models vary in their focus and theorization of them.

For example, solution-focused brief therapy (SFBT) has a strong emphasis on the construction of positive and growthful aspects of life and 'solution patterns', as in 3 above. SFBT works to achieve this partly through an intensive exploration and reappraisal of the instances in which solutions and resources are already present as exceptions to the times the problem occurs. The therapist makes a tactical assumption that even if 99 per cent of the client's life is dominated by problems, there will still be 1 per cent of the client's life that is concerned with other activities, experiences and ideas. The therapist invites the client to enhance the significance and performance of these constructive aspects of their life, and elaborate their structure and detail, rather than remain stuck in problem territory (de Shazer 1988, 1994). The client's defensive processes are relevant to therapeutic conversation only in so far as the client identifies them as being something they wish to see continue or happen more in their preferred future (Dolan 1991). Hence, a solution-focused therapist working with a client who cuts themselves as a defence against intolerable emotion in response to their peers – and who wants to stop cutting – is likely to focus more on the few times when the client does have positive interactions with their peers, or manages to stop by other means, rather than focus at length on the performance and effects of cutting for the client (Selekman 2002). A similar emphasis on exploring and restoring resourceful aspects of life might be adopted in systemic therapies with families who have become too preoccupied by managing a chronic illness or disability (e.g. Rolland 1995; Altschuler 1997), or in creative therapies with older persons whose lives have become restricted by an excessive focus on 'care' rather than quality of life and 'personhood' (e.g. Viney 1993; Kitwood 1997).

By contrast, cognitively oriented therapies are more likely to focus strongly on 2, developing better defences and placing risks in proportion, although with some attention to restoring non-problematic aspects of life, particularly if this can be framed as a form of coping strategy or reality checking. Cognitive-behavioural practice tends to be concerned with problem-solving and the resolution of misunderstandings of the self and the world. Defences could become an important focus for therapy if they form part of the problem-pattern that needs to be resolved (for example, if a defensive strategy of avoidance is used to manage anxiety arising from a phobia, which then serves to reinforce the phobia, since there is no opportunity to learn new ways to respond to or interpret the fear provoking situation). Otherwise, defences would not receive special attention distinct from any other psychological process. They might be studied to gather information about habitual patterns of thought, including distorted cognitions and other processing biases, but no more and no less than other kinds of thought and behaviour.

Psychotherapies which emphasize conflict as a key factor in psychological development and social interaction are more likely to place defences towards the heart of a therapy, whether to strengthen or revise these or to attempt to resolve some of the threats necessitating defences. This is the oldest tradition in psychotherapy as a distinct discipline, tracing its lineage back to Sigmund Freud's early work on drive theory and interpretation.

> What we experience as our minds, Freud suggests, is merely a small portion of it; the rest is by no means transparent to our feeble consciousness. The real meaning of much of what we think, feel, and do is determined unconsciously, outside our awareness. The mind has elaborate devices for regulating the instinctual tensions that are the source of all motivation and that exert a continuous pressure for discharge. The apparent transparency of mind is an illusion; the psyche and the personality are highly complex, intricately textured layers of instinctual impulses, transformations of those impulses, and defences against those impulses. Freud wrote: 'What we describe as a person's "character" is built up to a considerable extent from the material of sexual excitations and is composed of instincts that have been fixed since childhood, of constructions achieved by means of sublimation, and of other constructions, employed for effectively holding in check perverse impulses which have been recognised as being unutilizable' (1905d: 238–9). For Freud, the very stuff of personality is woven out of impulses and defences.
>
> (Mitchell and Black 1995: 16–17)

While Freud was initially fascinated by the secret and powerful material which needed to be repressed or hidden, later analysts continued this tradition through a more intensive focus on the means by which these operations were attempted, shifting the emphasis away from that which posed a risk (and so necessitated a defence), towards the nature of the defences themselves. Freud's daughter Anna pioneered this new territory (e.g. A. Freud 1936), shifting the emphasis away from aspects of the id towards a more encompassing interest in the operations of the mind as a whole, including the unconscious aspects of ego and superego functioning, and incorporating the idea that defences could be activated in relation to external threats, not simply id derivatives. Some strands of contemporary psychoanalytically informed therapy continue this focus on conflict management, and so prioritize the understanding and modification of defensive procedures as central to therapy.

Other therapies have come to emphasize the remediation of some hypothesized deficit which has hindered the client's self-development, rather than the resolution of conflicts. Within the psychoanalytic tradition, object relations theorists such as Fairbairn (1952) and Winnicott (e.g. 1965) believe that humans tended to organize themselves around relationships and attachments to other persons (they are 'object-seeking') rather than being motivated primarily by a hedonistic attempt to maximize pleasure and avoid pain/anxiety. Within the object-relations tradition, the therapeutic emphasis shifts towards the provision of a relational environment that is 'good enough' to allow the patient to develop a true self that can fully integrate the range of inner and outer experiences. This can then replace a 'false self' structure which distorts or neglects some aspects of experience in order to survive earlier inadequate caring (e.g. a baby that had to pretend to itself it was not unhappy in order not to provoke or overload a postnatally depressed mother).

Although the development of a false self can sometimes be regarded as a defence in its own right against a defective developmental environment, the analysis of the defence or false self *per se* is not primary in the clinical practice of object-relations theory (Greenberg and Mitchell 1983). Instead the emphasis is on the current provision of a positive intersubjective experience in which the therapist can be used by the patient to help to catalyse and structure a new self-organization. However, an understanding of the defences involved may be of use to the therapist in making sense of their own experience of being used by the patient – in supervision or through their own 'self-supervision' in the session – in order to tolerate and remain flexibly available to the client.

Person-centred therapy has a similar stance in relation to defences. Clinically, the emphasis is on the provision of a relational climate, providing the client with an experience of the 'core conditions' for therapeutic change and an unfolding of the true self (Rogers 1957; Lietaer 1984; compare Patterson 1984), rather than an analysis of the historic conditions of worth (such as whether or not conditional love was offered by primary carers). Although the client's defensive adaptation to distorting conditions of worth is seen as important in understanding current psychopathology (Rogers 1961), the clinical practice of person-centred therapy primarily concerns attempts to connect and support the client's innately trustworthy organismic valuing process and so develop their healthy true self, rather than direct challenges to dismantle or deconstruct the false self (Rogers 1951, 1989).

Other psychotherapies focus on the resolution of confusion, the clarification of desire and a search for authentic experience, and have a minimal focus on defences. Confusion or uncertainty itself may be understood as a danger in its own right. Personal construct psychotherapy in particular tends to conceptualize resistance and defences primarily in terms of operations to preserve and expand a person's capacity to understand and predict the world around them, 'as an expression of the client's continuing pursuit of an optimally predictive system' (Kelly 1955: 1050). Personal construct therapy assumes that clients are motivated to develop increasingly rich construct systems, which increase their capacity to predict and control themselves and their environment, and so generate a wider range of possibilities for action and understanding. Defensive processes will be invoked when something threatens to invalidate or disrupt a client's existing construct system, so that the client is faced with a loss of personal meaning (Fransella 1989, 1993). Conservatively, this might result in increasingly desperate attempts to hang on to the old way of construing the world; or more progressively to attempts to build a new construct system which can accommodate as much as possible of previous experience, but also help to orient the client constructively to current and future challenges (Fransella 2003).

The personal construct therapist aims to tread a careful balance between respecting the client's current perception of the apparent functions of their defences, and ultimately aiming to relieve the necessity of the client employing them. Rather than 'talking away' or dismantling the defences, the therapist aims to help the client to postpone interpretative closure of their experience and to remain productively in a 'liminal or betwixt and between' phase (Turner 1969) between the old system of understanding and a new way of construing, for long enough to develop a good range of alternative ways of understanding themselves and the world (this is Kelly's (1955) principle of 'constructive alternativism'). Personal construct therapists tend to understand defences as actions on the part of the client aimed at maintaining integrity of self, which may or may not be obviously associated with the presenting problem. The 'defence' in this sense is seen not as an absolute aspect of self, but as a balancing activity or a fragment of a complex construct system that is striving to maintain viability, integrity, comprehension and control of the events with which it (the construct system and therefore the person) is confronted (Liotti 1989). Like many of the humanistic therapies, personal construct therapy assumes that people will make wise choices out of the modes of understanding and relating available to them, but may initially present in therapy with a limited range of ways to be and to construe, and may attempt to resolve a liminal phase of uncertain (and hence anxious) construing so hastily that the new construct system offers few advantages. Premature 'tightening' of the personal construct system can itself be seen as a kind of counter-productive defence against anxiety.

Within the existential-phenomenological tradition (Spinelli 1994, 1996), the defensive attempt to evade the angst of authentic existence by the self-deception of living in 'bad faith' (Sartre 1956) creates confusion and self-alienation. It also provokes further anxiety and threat through the establishment of further distance and tension from the ongoing demands of situated 'being-in-the-world', which will inevitably continue to offer unavoidable and unpredictable real choices and dilemmas. As Spinelli (1994: 296) notes, even if only one option for living is viable a person might still approach this position in bad faith through an 'unwillingness to choose the one choice available' (see Boss 1967).

Maintaining the existential defence of an inauthentic self-structure runs the risk of further sedimenting or consolidating this, so producing new conflicts between one's being and one's doing, resulting in widening dis-ease and ontological insecurity (Laing 1960; Laing and Esterson 1964). However, from an existential-phenomenological stance the initial defence against existential angst was itself a confusion, since

existential choice emerges through the acceptance of the uncertainties that life presents us with. Angst, then, is not, properly speaking, a disturbing aspect of life which counselling psychologists must assist in alleviating, removing or resolving. Rather, angst exposes us to the possibilities and responsibilities of being – be they joyous or despairing, life-enhancing or confrontative of our eventual nothingness.

(Spinelli 1996: 185–6)

This suggests two important points about defences in psychotherapy: first, that they develop in response to apparent danger, not necessarily real risk, but also, second, that the risks emphasized by a therapist and their preferred theory may not correspond well to a client's hierarchy of dangers. Part of assessment for a psychotherapy should include a review of the correspondence between the kind of changes a client wants and the changes that a therapist hopes to support. Of course, the idea of defences and resistance which are outside conscious awareness renders any such assessment problematic, since a client's apparent reasons for wanting therapy may be read as a defensive distortion of their real motivations, while therapists cannot fully guarantee their own intentions in the encounter. None the less, it seems ethically crucial that therapists foster shared attempted discussion about the aims of therapy to try over time to build collaborative understandings.

Conclusion

We have suggested in this chapter that defences are processes and structures that seem to help to mediate protectively the relationship between something which is important yet vulnerable, and something else which poses an apparent threat to this. Different psychotherapies emphasize varying types of vulnerable element, and different kinds of threat. Family therapists may emphasize potential disruptions to a valued pattern of family life and the ways in which persons may interact together to counter these, whereas a personal construct therapist will concentrate on the individual's attempt to protect a personal construct system which enables them to predict and make sense of the world around them.

Some therapies focus on interpersonal or 'external' dangers and the client's attempts to respond or adapt to these, while the psychodynamic therapies in particular have explored how a person may feel so threatened by aspects of their own experience that these may then be hard to acknowledge or integrate. There are some similarities between the concept of defences and coping strategies in health psychology, but the construct of defences in psychotherapy is broader and includes many processes which are unconscious or outside everyday awareness.

We have also discussed in this chapter the importance of taking a developmental perspective on defences. Some defences persist long after the threat has disappeared, while other defences may arise in anticipation of danger yet to come. Over time, defences may come to serve other relational and psychological purposes besides the mediation of threat, and in so doing may have profound and enduring effects on the development of individuals, families and groups. Therapies vary in the degree to which they focus on past, present and future, and individual versus broader developmental histories, and this affects the nature of the defences each psychotherapy addresses.

Defences are widespread and manifold in everyday life, and are sometimes very helpful, sometimes not. Our next chapter continues this discussion in relation to a much more specific subset of defences, namely those which arise from the apparent risks of taking part in a therapy (whether as client or therapist) and the consequent attempts to avoid or eliminate such threat. Collectively, these can be called 'resistance'.

C H A P T E R   **5**

Resistance

Resistance is a clinical concept that refers to the myriad of methods a patient
uses to obstruct the very process that he is relying on to help him.
                                                        (Holmes and Bateman 1995: 163–4)

Defence and resistance

Defence is a broader term than resistance, and certainly not limited
to therapy. Resistance can be understood mainly as a 'subset' of
defence where the perceived (consciously or not) risk that is defended
against relates strongly to the therapeutic encounter and process,
rather than to some threat occurring outside the consulting room.
This resistance seems to have the potential to hinder or block the
therapeutic process. The perception of risk may or may not be accurate, and as this chapter discusses, therapy may sometimes actually be
enhanced by the resistance rather than impeded by it. By contrast,
barriers in therapy are not necessarily related to a perception of risk or
vulnerability.

Different therapies are likely to theorize different kinds of risk that
may provoke resistance. These may range from clients' resistance to
becoming aware of aspects of themselves which are painful, shameful
or confusing (as in psychodynamic therapies); or resistance to disclosing aspects of themselves which they fear may be judged harshly
or punitively by others (as in a person-centred therapy where the
client does not experience unconditional positive regard from the
therapist); or resistance to the undermining of existing structures of
understanding and prediction (as in personal construct therapy); or
resistance to changing patterns of behaviour and relations with
others through fear that worse problems would then arise (as in some
cognitive-behavioural therapy, or some behaviourally oriented family
therapies); through to resistance to being tutored or 'disciplined'
through therapy into a mode of being which is oppressive or

impoverishing, as in some feminist recastings of resistance (e.g. Gilligan *et al.* 1991; Weingarten 1995).

From the perspective of psychotherapies informed by ideas from feminism, critical theory and social justice, clients' problems can often be understood as expressions of protest or resistance against their treatment in the world, so that it would also be consistent and laudable to protest further against a therapy which simply attempts to return a client to the status quo ante. A woman who has been labelled 'depressed' and 'frigid' might well resist cooperation with a therapy which aims simply to restore her to 'normality', especially if she has become depressed as she has begun to recognize that 'normality' involves subjecting herself to exploitation and abuse by her partner. Discussing Freud's work with 'Dora' (Freud 1905b), the feminist writer Cixous (Cixous and Clement 1986) reconstructs Dora's hysterical symptoms as a revolt against patriarchal oppression, rather than demonstrating a pathology to be resolved. Billig (1999: Chapter 8) in turn examines Cixous's focus on this interpretation as a 'repression' of anti-Semitism as a key context for Dora's life. In emphasizing her feminist identification with Dora's oppression, Cixous manages to omit an analysis of her own relationship as a Jewish woman to the Jewish Dora's prolonged adoration of an image of the Christian Madonna in a predominant Christian society.

Levels of resistance

In most therapeutic contexts, there is often an expectation that one person or party (the client, family, team, organization, supervisee) is more in need of change than the other (the therapist, family therapy team, organizational consultant/manager, supervisor). Conventionally, the term resistance is usually applied to the person who, it is expected, should change most, although terms such as 'counter-resistance' (Schoenewolf 1993; Strean 1993) are sometimes used to refer to similar phenomena in which change seems to be sabotaged or disrupted by the therapist, supervisor or consultant. However, we take the view that all human relationships inevitably involve mutual influence and the possibility of change for both, and so prefer to avoid the term 'counter-resistance' in order not to privilege the view that clients necessarily need to change more than therapists.

Psychotherapies vary in the level of human systems that they attempt to address in therapy. For example, while a cognitive therapist might focus on an individual client's apparent non-compliance, the Milan Associates' family therapy (e.g. Selvini-Palazzoli *et al.* 1978, 1980) focuses strongly on resistance by family units against therapeutic teams. The Just Therapy team in New Zealand (Waldegrave 1990) emphasizes the importance of mobilizing change in wider social systems, including whole communities and political structures. These variations affect the way in which resistance is conceptualized as operating at certain levels, such as the individual, dyadic, family/ group or societal/discursive.

One important dimension of difference between psychotherapies concerns the extent to which resistance is understood as a property within a particular individual (or group), versus resistance being understood as a kind of activity, process or relationship between persons (or groups). In the former more individualistic or 'diagnostic' frame, it appears to make sense to speak of a 'resistant client' or 'resistant family', as though this reflects a relatively stable aspect of their personality or style. In the latter frame resistance is understood as something being called forth and expressed through the joint participation of the 'resistor' (e.g. a family) and 'resisted' (e.g. a clinic) performing a certain kind of relationship. This latter position is potentially more generative for therapists, since it implies that the way the therapist participates in the therapeutic relationship can make a difference.

The construct of resistance can also be used to refer to similar dynamics and issues between psychotherapy trainees and trainers, between supervisees and supervisors or between therapists and their organizational contexts. (Indeed, therapeutic organizations may themselves sometimes be seen as 'resistant' to pressures for change arising from clinical, research or social situations: see Skynner 1989; Obholzer and Roberts 1994; Campbell 2000.) Writers on supervision have sometimes emphasized the resistance of supervisees to supervisors, and, less frequently, resistance by the supervisor against the supervisee's attempts to invite them to work or change in certain ways (Feltham 2000). The field remains divided about the extent to which supervision should be seen as involving substantially different skills and processes from therapy, and about the degree to which psychotherapy training resembles personal development processes through therapy (Carroll 1996; Feltham 2000). We prefer an inclusive stance, and Chapter 6 includes a further review of defensive, resistance processes in supervision and professional development.

Resistance in perspective

Resistance concerns apparently counter-productive processes, hindering an attempted process of beneficial influence within a therapeutic context, which ranges from a relationship between individuals in therapy through to attempting change in the functions of a psychotherapeutic institution. As with defences more broadly, we suggest therapists should read resistance as perspectival: that is, whether it constitutes real resistance or not, whether it is seen as problematic or desirable, depends upon the position of the person making this judgement, and perhaps also upon the power of that person to impose their perspective on others.

To draw an analogy with power and resistance outside therapy, organizations such as Hamas in the Middle East may be seen as terrorists or freedom fighters, depending on the observer's stance in relation to Israeli/Palestinian politics. The 'resistance of Hamas to subjugation by the Israeli state', which could be redefined as 'extremist terrorism against innocent Israelis', can be seen as deplorable or laudable depending on the observer's position. Some observations, such as those of the USA, carry more weight on the world stage than those of others, such as Yemen. Holding both interpretations in mind simultaneously may be difficult, given the intensely emotive nature of the issues involved and strong pressures to take sides rather than tolerate a multiperspectival view.

Some observers, particularly those who wish to bring the weight of their opinion to bear on those who differ from them, may assert that their perspective is more valid than another's view, or even attempt to disqualify the possibility that there can be other interpretations besides their own dominant version, by punishing or marginalizing dissenting voices. Ferenczi's exclusion from Freud's favoured inner circle can be understood as an act of resistance by Freud against the anxiety invoked by Ferenczi's threatening insistence that patients' distress reflected real abuse and trauma rather than intrapsychic fantasy and conflict (Ferenczi 1932; Masson 1985a); or it can be regarded as a benign defence – in the best interests of analysands – of emerging psychoanalytic rigour and clinical sophistication against the heretical Ferenczi's potentially corrosive conceptual errors. The views that we ourselves express could be understood as misrepresenting or denying the 'real' meaning and significance of resistance in psychotherapy by readers wishing to defend or promote a particular therapeutic ideology. To contrast two extremes, from a solution-focused perspective, this text is redundant since resistance is an unnecessary concept, while from an orthodox analytic stance our own views are hopelessly naive, lacking the detail necessary for understanding the intricacies of resistance and its management.

Within psychotherapeutic discourse, attempts to assert a particular perspective on resistance are often framed within an ethical discourse regarding 'benefit to clients' ('If you don't see it this way, you won't be helping your clients very well') rather than as appeals to institutional or theoretical loyalties alone. Within such discourse, some commentators may value resistance and approaches to resistance according to their success or failure in achieving particular ends, while others may emphasize ethics in which the very act of resistance and therapeutic ways of relating to this have their own (im)moral worth, regardless of eventual outcome.

In the psychoanalytic traditions, it is essential to monitor and respond to resistance, since clients' ideas and actions to pursue well-being cannot be taken at face value, because of the dynamic and conflictual unconscious. Patients may say they are happy when they are not, may say that they are ready to end therapy when they are not really ready and so on. Failure to attend to such possibilities could constitute a naive lapse of professional responsibility by the therapist. From a feminist perspective, however, the very idea that therapists (often male, and in relatively privileged positions in patriarchal institutional structures such as state services) assume that when a client (often female, and in relatively subordinate positions in the relationship) says 'no' she may really mean 'yes' is a disturbing reflection of a patriarchal dynamic in which men exercise power to define women's experiences and wishes for them:

> Forrester argues that the psychoanalytic situation is one of unequal power, as the analyst metaphorically seduces the analysand, refusing to accept the latter's accounts of themselves. Moreover, as Forrester points out, the majority of Freud's earliest patients were women and all subsequent analyses by Freudian analysts are, in some form or another, repetitions of Freud's original cases. Thus analysis is founded on the image of the male seducer, taking the woman's 'no' for 'yes'.
>
> (Billig 1999: 199–200; citing Forrester 1990)

We are not suggesting that this problem is specific to psychoanalytic practice. The broader point is that psychotherapy involves relationships of power, difference and inequality, and this will affect the way in which meanings are attributed in therapy. Explicitly or not, psychotherapies invite persons to construe their lives in terms of the assumptive frameworks and metaphors informing the conduct of the therapy (for example, in cognitive-behavioural rhetoric that 'thoughts', 'feelings' and 'behaviours' are distinct, or in humanistic therapies that there is a 'true self'). In so doing therapies run the risk of alienating persons from their own lived experience and commitments in the world (e.g. Perkins 1991). There is inevitably some difference between the psychological models used by the therapist and the 'folk psychology' and self-understandings of the client (Bruner 1990; White 2001). Too little difference and therapy may have little effect, too much and either the client's identity is colonized by the therapeutic model or the therapy is rejected. Masson (1993) and many other critics of mainstream psychotherapies have argued that the concept of 'resistance' is widely used by therapists to dismiss or marginalize the views of clients who fail to adopt a subordinate position to the professional (for example, to justify increasingly oppressive treatment to 'overcome' their resistance, or conversely to excuse abandoning a client who is too difficult).

Resistance may also be apparent to one participant but not to another, as a reflection of insufficiently understood differences about the purpose and direction of a therapy, or more broadly because of significant differences between client and therapist about values and goals in life (Aponte 1985; Falicov 1995). For example, the value of being separate and autonomous from one's parent(s) in adult life has a higher priority in some cultures and some families than others (Triandis 1995; Owusu-Bempah 2002), but can be taken for granted by many Western therapists. A structural family therapist from a community which privileges such separation and autonomy may be frustrated by the resistance of a family from a different culture to engage in helping a troubled adolescent to move on and develop more independence, particularly if the therapist fails to recognize that the family places a different priority on this compared to other goals. Working to overcome such resistance could constitute an inadvertent act of colonialism if the therapist is successful in making some or all of the family conform to the therapist's preferred family values. Similarly, a therapist who is organized by a belief from their own family-of-origin (Byng-Hall 1995), perhaps compounded by their professional training, that open communication is healthy may experience as resistant a family who have chosen to conceal some facts about biological parentage, such as intrafamilial informal adoption, from their children. The therapist may attempt to persuade the family to disclose these secrets to the children, with the family then feeling misunderstood and threatened, and so closing ranks. The therapist might then interpret this as further confirmation that the secret-keeping is problematic and redouble the effort to push the family towards disclosure.

The apparently counter-productive nature of resistance may also concern the time frame for evaluation. Something which seems problematic to either therapist or client at a given time may later turn out to be very helpful. A therapist may feel they have sufficient clinical experience and expectation to gauge that it is ultimately likely to be helpful to the client to challenge the client's resistance over an issue, but the therapist cannot know this in advance for a specific client. Equally, another therapist might believe it is more ethical to accept a client's resistance as a valid feedback that a certain therapeutic avenue should be discontinued, even though this is contrary to their clinical experience with other clients and their knowledge of an external evidence base. However, what seems right for that client today may turn out to be profoundly unhelpful next month; perhaps the therapist was remiss in not trying harder to convince the client to persevere with something in the therapy that was difficult. Therapy inevitably involves ethical risk-taking, balancing the therapist's experience and expertise with that of clients, who can also be presumed to know something about themselves (Krause 2002).

Regulation and normalization versus growth or development

We have argued in the preceding section that mismatches or misunderstandings regarding the aims of therapy can be an important source of resistance. An important dichotomy between therapeutic aims concerns

- emphasis on functional adaptation to circumstances or restoration of function/previous status/symptomatic relief ('regulation' and homeostasis); versus
- focus on emancipation from constraints, growth into something new, and the subversion of prevailing circumstances ('resistance' to dominant discourses, or growth).

There are tensions within the extended family of psychotherapies between therapy as a form of regulation where the therapist exercises a 'normalizing authority' or 'restorative function' to provide symptomatic relief and help clients to function 'normally', and therapy itself as a form of resistance with a more radical intent (Burman *et al.* 1996). Resistance in this sense means an emancipatory struggle against impoverishing or oppressive modes of life imposed by one's self and/ or by others. Such therapies do not aim to help clients to get 'back on track' or 'back to normal life', since the expression of a problem and/or the decision to enter therapy can be construed as an initiative to move away from, not back to, life-as-it-was. Although the humanistic therapies frame this in less politicized language, these growth-oriented psychotherapies assume that the therapist is trying to help clients to develop towards a different way of being more congruent with their real self, rather than attempting to restore clients to old ways of being.

Tensions between psychotherapy as a mode of regulation or as a means of resistance and radicalism are not simply a reflection of competing schools of therapy, nor a question confined to overtly politicized paradigms such as feminist psychotherapy. They are often in play within the same model, as Burton and Davey note in relation to the psychodynamic paradigm:

> One important concept that emerges from the idea of defence is that of patient compliance . . . this issue is crucial to an understanding of the possibilities of cure and the extent to which the task of therapy is compliance to the normalizing authority of the therapist. If what ails people is precisely how the demands of society impact upon their lives to define them in ways that deny their difference and diversity it may well be that the body and symptoms become a method of both expressing dis-ease but at the same time of distancing the self from its implication by declaring one's problems medical. Psychodynamics is often torn between a desire to hitchhike on the status and esteem of the medical model of mental illness and the more radical deconstructive challenge that suggests we are trapped precisely by a vision of ourselves that splits off unacceptable parts or declares them alien from our being.
>
> (Burton and Davey 1996: 120–1)

Such tensions may also be apparent where a therapist with a more radical agenda is funded by an agency with regulatory or restorative aims (as when a psychoanalyst works within a state-funded hospital, or when a feminist therapist works within a biomedically oriented eating disorders clinic). This may be reflected in unease and confusion surrounding appropriate measures for the evaluation of effectiveness in such settings (e.g. Elliott 1998; Perron 1999).

Some of this debate revolves around therapists' trust in the beneficence or otherwise of the established dominant social conditions, and
therapists' relative emphasis on the ethics of client autonomy and
minimalist intervention versus relational ethics of collaborative
empowerment and cooperation. For example, strategic and cognitive-
behavioural therapists tend to share an ethical stance that values brief
intervention as a way of maximizing client autonomy and choice,
and where it is preferable to be guided by a client's explicit stated aims
for therapy rather than deconstruct these at length. This stance makes
sense given a basic trust in the relative beneficence and transparency
of social life and a libertarian belief that individual citizens exercise
wise choices as long as they are not excessively hampered by specific
problems such as mental illness. Restoring a client to a position well
adapted to function in current social circumstances seems an ethical
and logical goal for such therapy, promoting normal functioning so
that the citizen can make good use of other personal resources and
social structures outside therapy. By contrast, therapists who have less
faith in the pre-eminence of conscious rational thought might be
much less inclined to take their clients' stated aims for therapy at face
value, and therapists who view the social order as impoverished or
unjust (at least to their clients) are unlikely to be content with a normalizing therapy.

Some therapies (such as cognitive-behavioural, strategic and solution-focused therapies) which emphasize focus on a task, and on the
working alliance mode of the therapeutic relationship, tend to frame
difficulties and setbacks in the therapeutic process primarily in terms
of non-compliance, or as a misfit between the ways of working preferred by therapists and clients (so, for instance, a client may not carry
out homework simply because the therapist did not explain it clearly,
or because the therapist failed to consider sufficiently whether the
client actually had sufficient skills and resources to undertake the
homework in the first place). Effectively, these therapies reframe
resistance as a kind of barrier relating to confusion and misunderstandings, clumsy practice or a need for revised case formulation,
rather than as a defence relating to perceived threats and potential
conflict of agenda between therapist and client. Task-oriented therapies tend to draw upon a metaphor of resistance to do with movement,
momentum and inertia, force and friction. The image invoked is of
the therapist pushing or pulling the client over uneven terrain; at
times the going seems particularly tough so that it seems there is a
need for more force, extra lubrication or new wheels, or negotiation
of a detour or new destination, or perhaps more patience.

Freud's own preferred metaphors for psychic processes were mainly military, as though the movement in question were a struggle to control territory (the unconscious). Many psychodynamic therapies tend to be closely wedded to conflictual interpretations, although some analysts such as Winnicott significantly extend psychodynamic ideas through detailed theorization of healthy psychological development, including maturational and healing processes to leaven the apparently pervasive pathologization of mental life suggested by some readings of early psychoanalysis. Humanistic and cognitive-behavioural therapies have more ambiguous stances, with movement being understood less as conflict and more as growth towards something greater or transcendent in the humanistic tradition, or as a problem-solving journey towards a determined destination, as the metaphor of non-compliance implies.

By contrast, feminist and postmodern discursive and critical therapies, loosely characterized as 'collaborative therapies' (e.g. White and Epston 1990; Gilligan *et al.* 1991; Hoffman 1993; Anderson 1997), place much greater emphasis on co-constructing shared understandings to bridge communication and relational gulfs, and often explicitly repudiate the use of militaristic or conflictual metaphors and language as perpetuating heteropatriarchal power relations (Gilligan 1982). However, the concept of resistance is sometimes invoked in relation to political metaphors of identity, autonomy and occupation or colonization, so that some collaborative therapists see themselves as supporting their clients' resistance against other oppressive forces. This is consistent with the use of 'externalization' practices in narrative therapy (Carey and Russell 2002), in which therapists assume that a person's life is separate from the problem affecting them, rather than treating a person's self or self-structure as the problem. In feminist therapies, the particular resistance privileged for attention is often the struggle against hierarchical forms of domination and inequality, associated with patriarchy, such as sexism and racism.

Some theorists within more mainstream psychotherapy models might argue that this feminist/collaborative politicized understanding of resistance is not really resistance, and that the core concept of resistance by a client to a therapist's intervention has been lost or misunderstood, perhaps as an immature denial of the difficult dynamics of therapeutic relationships. However, this argument lays bare the radical intent of critical or discursively oriented psychotherapies, which may deliberately subvert or co-opt conventional psychotherapy terminology like resistance into new usages as an act of resistance against models of the person and of psychotherapy which are seen as part of the problem. The argument revolves around the degree to which psychotherapy and psychotherapeutic psychologies should be seen as positive and emancipatory, neutral tools or potentially oppressive knowledge, the apparently benevolent application of which may have harmful or dehumanizing effects that should be resisted.

Therapeutic attitudes towards resistance

The term resistance tends to conjure up connotations of agency, wilfulness, deliberate action and choice in relation to therapy, in a way that other kinds of defence or barrier need not. This means that issues of blame and responsibility may often be involved in a way that is emotionally loaded for clients, therapists, supervisors and trainers. It is one thing for a client not to attend an appointment because they missed their bus, but quite another if the therapist interprets this as a comment on the pace of the therapy or the quality of the therapeutic relationship. This emotionally charged meaning is seen by some therapists as signalling the importance of theorizing resistance, while other therapists see this as good reason to avoid, minimize or abandon the construct in favour of non-compliance or 'stasis' (Dryden and Trower 1989). Solution-focused therapists believe that resistance is an unhelpful concept best avoided in favour of greater therapist flexibility; if the client seems resistant, this should be taken to mean that the therapist should find better ways to cooperate with the client (de Shazer 1984; Davy 2003). Although this seems a productive rationale for de-emphasizing resistance, it can also be read as a defensive manoeuvre to avoid the therapist's own pain of acknowledging that he or she is unhelpful, unwelcome or unable to alleviate distress for some clients. Personal construct therapists understand therapist resistance in terms of the theoretical construct of hostility. Imbued in this notion is the therapist's refusal to give up an ineffective line of inquiry or therapeutic strategy, in order to maintain a view of himself or herself, paradoxically, as effective (Kelly 1955). The concept of resistance can be used to blame clients for therapeutic failure, but abandoning the concept altogether may mean that therapeutic failure is overlooked and forgotten.

What counts as resistance depends very much on the flexibility and breadth of the therapist's skills, and on the therapist's conceptualization of what is therapeutic. Hence, one important approach to resistance is to develop a broader view of therapy so that a disciplined choice can be exercised between ways of relating to the concept of resistance. Three main options are available. These are:

- preventing resistance from occurring (and/or ignoring it as far as possible);
- overcoming resistance;
- making use of resistance.

Preventing or minimizing resistance

Therapists can try to overlook or ignore resistance, concentrating instead on what seems productive and possible, doing more of what works, rather than analysing and addressing what seems difficult or blocked. A therapist may simply choose to ignore a client's persistent late arrival for therapy sessions and concentrate on using the remaining time as efficiently as possible. Alternatively, the therapist may choose to theorize their work with such a client through a model which does not emphasize boundaries, non-verbal communication, hidden meaning and so on, so that persistent lateness is not interpreted as resistance to the therapy. This could be a useful tactical posture if the therapist has noticed a developing tendency on their own part to blame or punish the client for late arrivals. Deliberately choosing to reinterpret the client's actions in a framework which minimizes negative connotations might help to sustain a warmer and more constructive relationship between therapist and client. However, this choice obviously precludes other possible ways of responding to the lateness (and the therapist's mounting irritation) as a therapeutic resource or opportunity, as we discuss below.

If the therapist chooses to understand the lateness as a form of resistance, a related possibility is to try to prevent resistance by 'trouble-shooting' or problem-solving to find ways to avoid provoking this. The therapist might ask the client if there is a more convenient time to schedule sessions, or the therapist could decide to halve the length of sessions if the client only turns up for the second half. Alternatively, the therapist might assume that the client's lateness reflects a misunderstanding about how the therapy might be conducted, or about the original contract, and either offer some further explanation about therapy or renegotiate the therapeutic contract.

Apparent resistance might indicate that a client is being invited to do something in therapy which they actually do not understand, or do not have the skills to accomplish. A therapist who tries to conduct a 90-minute conversational interview with a small child in a dull room with no toys or play materials may find that they have severely overestimated the child's verbal skills and attention span in that situation. Preventing resistance requires an analysis of what is currently being asked of the client, and how this does or does not fit with his or her current capacities, and then changing what is expected of the client. If a client persistently fails to carry out diary-keeping homework tasks between sessions, it is possible that the therapist has overestimated the client's literacy skills, or failed to appreciate how chaotic and busy their home life is.

Similar considerations may apply to apparent resistance in supervision. A supervisor might notice that a supervisee turns up late, consistently fails to present their case sufficiently clearly and coherently in supervision, runs out of time to discuss cases which they had told the supervisor they needed to discuss and fails to make use of clinical ideas that the supervisor has offered in previous sessions. While this could be construed as resistance to the supervisory process (see Ladany *et al.* 1996; Lawton 1996), it could also be taken as a cue for the supervisor to: (a) renegotiate a more convenient supervision time or provide specific advice on time-management; (b) give clearer guidelines for case presentations, or offer more active support of case presentations in supervision through questions and summarizing; (c) take a more proactive role in time-keeping during the supervision; or (d) seek some further consultation or training about supervisory skills to find more effective ways of sharing clinical ideas.

Preventing resistance might also mean checking and accepting that there are some things the client (or supervisee etc.) does not wish to do. If the therapist can accept that the client has always hated homework and does not want to do any, the therapist can avoid resistance by not setting homework in the first place. If a client has said that they do not want therapy to 'rake up things that have happened in my past which I would rather forget', the therapist might sidestep resistance by interviewing with a strong present and future focus.

Personal construct therapy assumes that there is a basic human need to predict life experiences and give meaning to them, and that resistance arises from a reluctance to move in the direction of a personal world of decreased meaning. Hence, any goal must be made meaningful before a client will move towards it. Attempting to develop new understandings or constructs about the self and the world runs the risk of unsettling existing meanings. This is likely to result in resistance unless the therapist can, first, offer a clear explanation of how a phase of greater uncertainty might actually lead towards a meaningful higher order goal valued by the client, and, second, sustain a conversational climate in which new understandings can be considered on an 'as if' basis, so that they can be developed without immediately displacing the security of current constructs, which are to be merely suspended for a time. The assumption is that generating new options through this 'constructive alternativism' (Kelly 1955) is less likely to evoke resistance than attempts to replace directly, block, undermine or change an existing way of being. 'Arguing that a person will resist changing in a direction which leads to a less meaningful way of life results in personal construct psychotherapy being largely directed toward sculpting the future rather than demolishing the problem in the present or exploring the past' (Fransella 1989: 24). Using a tentative 'as if', 'supposing that' or 'yes-and' rather than 'either-or' style of thinking is a common broad strategy across constructivist and constructionist psychotherapies for minimizing resistance. The therapeutic challenge is to find ways in which the client can experience a 'safe uncertainty' (Mason 1993).

Cognitive-behavioural therapists tend to be interested in resistance phenomena primarily in order to prevent or eliminate them (e.g. Leahy 2001), and to maximize compliance and effective treatment. To reflect this collaborative and task-focused aspiration, rather than the conflictual or 'threat' derived meaning of resistance in other therapies, the term resistance is often rejected by cognitive-behavioural therapists in favour of the term 'non-compliance'. Authors such as Dryden and Trower (1989) argue from a cognitive-behavioural perspective that the concept of resistance is a rationalization that is used to explain away failure which is in fact the therapist's fault. This view highlights how therapists' theoretical positions may themselves operate as defensive processes, protecting therapists and their preferred working practices from the risk of criticism.

Cognitive-behavioural therapy promotes a collaborative, working partnership between therapist and client, but one where therapists are assumed to have particular expert knowledge founded on empirical evidence about functional versus dysfunctional patterns of thinking, feeling and behaving, and expert knowledge about problem-solving strategies. The nature of the collaboration is thus for the client to help the therapist to understand the nature of their problem and the contexts in which it has arisen so that an individual 'case formulation' can be made (e.g. Persons 1989; Bruch and Bond 1998; Tarrier and Calam 2002). The client also needs to cooperate with the therapist in conducting behavioural and/or thought experiments to test out alternative strategies, and to gather further data for iterative reformulation. The aims and values of the cognitive therapist are not placed centre-stage as in need of examination or revision by the client and the encounter. The client's phenomenology and values are of interest, but primarily in order to understand and resolve potential difficulties in helping the client to use and relate to cognitive-behavioural principles.

Preventing or minimizing resistance can require careful assessment of relatively complex capacities. A supervisee might appear to be resistant to working on issues relating to a client's sexual identity, and equally find it hard to consider or address such themes in their supervision (McCann *et al.* 2000). One possibility is that it is the supervisee who is still struggling with their own sexual identity. The supervisor might need to choose between: (a) ignoring the resistance and working on other themes instead, trusting that the consequences for the clients will be relatively insignificant; (b) offering some theoretical framework for thinking about sexuality in therapy that might make it a more manageable topic for the supervisee; and (c) pressing the supervisee to undertake some personal development work to help them to clarify their own position.

It can be argued that some attempts to ignore or prevent resistance actually allow resistance to dominate the therapeutic relationship and possibilities. If a woman feels forced to organize her daily life around largely successful attempts to placate a volatile and physically abusive partner, this does not mean that there is no fear and violence in their relationship. It is not uncommon for therapists working with clients who, they fear, may be aggressive to stick to safe topics to avoid provoking resistance and retaliation. This may incapacitate the therapy and fail the client. Therapists working with children may find that some carers seem very reluctant to allow the therapist to talk with the children without the carer present. Cooperating by agreeing to stick to family or parent/carer work only may seem to forestall this resistance, but perhaps at a cost of denying a child the opportunity to make a disclosure of abuse.

Therapists working with abusive men often find that they seem resistant to accepting responsibility for their actions. Ignoring such resistance appears to be unethical to many therapists, who may emphasize overcoming it. However, an intermediate position is to conduct some developmental work first, to elicit the competencies and skills that the client already has in taking responsibility and thinking ethically in at least some aspects of their lives; having prepared this platform of a caring and responsible identity they can then be invited to think further about responsibility for abusive actions (and possibilities for restitution). For instance, the therapist might invite the client to remember and describe someone in their own childhood who had valued and protected them when they were in distress. Then, the therapist might invite the client to reflect on their own abusive actions through the understanding eyes of that earlier protector. What would that protector say about the importance of taking adult responsibility, and how might that caring protector think about the significance and meaning of the client being able to acknowledge the harm of abuse and exercise more responsibility now (Jenkins 1990; Law 1999)? Preparing an alternative caring position from which the client can reflect on their actions and the effects on the abused person can reduce the resistance which is likely when abusers are asked to address their actions.

Overcoming resistance

Overcoming resistance is an alternative important therapeutic posture, which may be adopted either because attempts to prevent resistance were unsuccessful or because the therapeutic model sees challenge or resolution of resistance as an important mutative process; in this latter position preventing resistance in the first place might be seen as unhelpful.

Overcoming resistance may involve relatively active or confrontational approaches (e.g. Janov 1973; Bergman 1985; Danvaloo 1987), or slower, more reflective means, which aim to dissolve the underpinnings of the resistance rather than overthrow it forcefully. Person-centred therapy assumes that a degree of resistance to the therapeutic process is probably inevitable, reflecting the extent to which clients are able to experience themselves as being offered the core conditions of warmth, empathy, non-judgemental/unconditional positive regard and congruence by the therapist (Rogers 1957; compare Patterson 1984). As an ordinary human being, the therapist will never be able to provide these conditions perfectly because their own fears and needs (such as a need to be liked) or their theories of human behaviour (for example, that bereaved people will feel sad) may become blocks to empathy. Mearns and Thorne (1988: 55) suggest that a belief that a client will experience a given situation in the same way as the therapist is a particular hazard leading to 'false empathy'. The client's experience of the conditions being offered by the therapist will inevitably be distorted or shaped to some degree by the client's internalized conditions of worth. The client's resistance to change in decreasing the risk posed by change, but by highlighting the benefits of change. This might involve a systematic 'cost–benefit' analysis of the risks and rewards of change versus no change: for example, using structured approaches like 'motivational interviewing' (Miller and Rollnick 1991). Sometimes, however, this review may suggest that the current goal should not be to help a client actually to make a particular change, but may relate to an earlier preparatory stage of exploring the implications of such a change if they were to decide to implement it, and how this might be done. This approach to overcoming resistance is similar to personal construct psychotherapy's emphasis on a climate of propositionality, in which changes can be considered without commitment, with current ways of being suspended but not abandoned.

The context for a psychotherapy may be an important influence on the cost–benefit analysis. This can be particularly evident when working with mandated clients: for example, with offenders required to attend a multisystemic therapy programme (Henggeler 1999) to avoid custodial sentences, or with parents who are required to undergo 'treatment' for their abusive behaviour before a court will consider allowing them to see their children again. The client's goals may be very different from those of the therapist's agency, but the therapist can remind the client of the referral reasons and the consequences of failing to change, in order to push the client's 'cost–benefit' analysis towards active participation in change. However, overcoming resistance in this way runs the risk of inadvertently reinforcing some of the original problems precipitating referral, since the client may experience reconfirmation that coercion and threat are a useful and now societally validated means of achieving goals. Therapists in such settings need to tread a shifting line between assertive clarity and realistic presentation of options on the one hand, and on the other drifting into coercive practice, replicating the pathology of clients and/or of the criminal justice system.

Attempts to overcome resistance may be explicitly named as such in a collaborative manner; but they can also be implemented more covertly or unilaterally by the therapist, so that the client is unaware that the therapist considers them resistant, and is not told the therapist's reasons for suggesting certain actions or conversations that the therapist hopes will overcome resistance. (We have even heard of a Kleinian analyst who raised the fee for a persistently late patient!) Some family therapists have been influenced by ideas that problem symptoms may have a positive homeostatic function in stabilizing a family situation (such as the impending breakdown of a person-centred therapy represents a shifting balance between the capacity to apply their organismic valuing process to their own sel and contradictory pulls and messages from an evaluation of thei self-esteem or distorted self-image, according to their internalized conditions of worth (Rogers 1961). Person-centred therapy aims to overcome this process through a kind of gentle dissolution, in which the consistent and prolonged provision of the core conditions acts as a solvent which dissolves away the conditions of worth, which Lietaer (1984) calls 'counterconditioning', and provides a supportive environment nourishing the client's organismic valuing process (Rogers 1957; Patterson 1984; Tudor 2000).

By contrast, some therapies which emphasize debate and argument with clients, such as rational-emotive behaviour therapy (e.g. Dryden 1990) and some forms of existential and philosophical therapy (e.g. van Deurzen-Smith 1988), adopt a more direct confrontational approach to overcoming resistance, such as utilizing Socratic questions to lead the client towards a demonstration of the folly of their initial beliefs, or pointing out the client's apparently resistive manoeuvres and asking the client to explain how these are consistent with their stated aims.

Cognitive-behavioural therapies are less reliant on confrontational approaches, but nevertheless tend to use direct, explicit approaches to address resistance or non-compliance, naming it and posing it as a shared problem. For example, the therapist might share a perception that the client is not complying with the therapeutic process and express curiosity about this, and then: (a) attempt to problem-solve to see if there are practical problems/blocks which can be removed; (b) revisit the treatment rationale; (c) review the treatment contract to see if the correct goals have been chosen; and (d) explore ways to examine and/or enhance the client's motivation to change towards the goals specified (e.g. Leahy 2001).

A distinction can be made between conducting such reviews in order to try to make the client less resistant to the current therapy, and adapting the therapy to fit more closely the client's current interests and motivation. The latter approach is probably better under-stood as preventing (rather than overcoming) resistance by adoptin; goals and approaches which seem less threatening. Transtheoretica 'stages of change' models such as those of Prochaska and DiClement (1992) would frame this as minimizing resistance by reviewing th 'customer' status or readiness to change of the client, and adaptii the therapy offered accordingly.

The former option attempts to overcome resistance not

marriage), so that at least some family members may try to avoid therapy to avoid the risks of change. A therapist who believes that a particular family member is benefiting from the maintenance of a current problem might decline to offer a session until that family member has committed to attend, or might double the interval between sessions if either an appointment is cancelled or the family arrives without that particular member (Haley 1963; Selvini-Palazzoli *et al.* 1978).

The ethical question of whether the end justifies the means is an important consideration in such choices. At one extreme, a therapist may feel that the initial therapeutic contract to achieve some speci-fied change constitutes an encompassing mandate to use whatever means necessary to help the client to achieve the goal, with failure to accept the therapeutic authority derived from this mandate constitut-ing an abdication of professional responsibility. Strategic therapists (e.g. Bergman 1985; Haley 1996) have argued this position, claiming that it is more ethical for therapists to acknowledge and use their power in the therapeutic relationship, accepting responsibility for exercising it in the client's overall 'best interest', rather than pretend-ing the relationship is an equal one, or resorting to subtle but power-ful rhetorical means of influencing clients, where therapist and client deceive themselves that such processes are not in play (Kogan 1998; Guilfoyle 2002).

Advocates of approaches which actively attempt to overcome client resistance without explicit agreement – such as strategic therapy, primal therapy (Janov 1973), Milan family therapy (Selvini-Palazzoli *et al.* 1978; Boscolo *et al.* 1987) and Danvaloo's (1987, 1990) short-term analytic therapy – tend to believe that the therapist has a more accurate understanding of the problem than the client; this is perhaps combined with a belief that if the therapist reveals this understanding too early it might allow the client more time to construct an even stronger resistance to neutralize the therapeutic interventions. The therapist assumes that clients do not always (consciously) know what is in their own best interests, and may have very mixed feelings about therapy. Ethically, the therapist's stance is to be an advocate for that part of the client which is in favour of change, even at times when other aspects of the client are more to the fore.

Some family therapists work in teams, with colleagues observing behind a one-way mirror and then consulting with the therapist in a break away from the family. This way of working involves the idea of back up from a team to help to overcome a family's resistance to change. Such models assume that family processes of resistance can include attempts to induct or seduce the therapist into colluding with the family's current way of being, thus preventing the therapist from making a useful difference (Selvini-Palazzoli *et al.* 1978; Boscolo *et al.* 1987). Colleagues behind the mirror may be able to identify such collusive processes, retrieve the therapist from participation in these and make suggestions for intervention to disrupt homeostatic processes, such as paradoxical injunctions not to change, or positive connotations of the current problem pattern.

Critics of such approaches argue that they justify potential abuses of power by the therapist, and ignore the importance of informed consent as an ongoing process, rather than as an initial hurdle. They suggest that relational ethics (Gilligan 1982; McNamee and Gergen 1999), valuing clients as partners in change and respecting client autonomy, should be given at least equal weight to concerns about outcome. Critics of strategic and confrontational approaches to overcoming resistance also argue that it is naive to believe that the therapist has a privileged position of expertise, allowing them to know what is best for the client(s). The risk of misunderstanding what an apparent resistance may be about, or failing to appreciate what either might be useful for the client or may feel dangerous for the client, can be particularly pronounced when there are significant differences between therapist and client, such as cultural issues relating to gender, class, 'race' and ethnicity, (dis)ability, age and sexual orientation (see, for instance, Falicov 1995; Ridley 1995; Krause 2002; Mason and Sawyerr 2002). Too much psychotherapy has involved middle- or upper-class white male therapists theorizing about ways in which clients from less privileged groups should be helped to live a good life as defined by the therapist and their theory.

Contemporary family/systemic therapy has moved away from expert approaches, which explicitly aim to influence clients in a direction determined by the therapist, and now favours collaborative stances in which therapists aim to assist clients to develop their own ways forward (e.g. Hoffman 1993; Anderson 1997). Therapists using these approaches may still work with teams, but they conceptualize the team's function as contributing a greater variety of ideas and observations for consideration by the family and therapist (e.g. Andersen 1990; White 1997), rather than as a defence for the therapist against a hostile or resistant family process. However, it is still debatable how much clients are fully informed about the theoretical premises for these collaborative therapies, and how much this shift conceals therapist power rather than levels the playing field (e.g. Guilfoyle 2002; Legg and Stagaki 2002).

Making use of resistance

Some therapists aim to ignore, prevent or overcome resistance. These postures are united by the idea that resistance constitutes a problem in psychotherapy, or at best is an unnecessary distraction. However, it is also possible to see instances of apparent resistance as resources and opportunities which can enhance the psychotherapeutic process. Several variants of this are possible:

- resistance can be understood as further rich information about clients, their problems/resources and ways of managing difficulties;
- resistance can be understood as feedback about the therapy that the therapist can use to modify the conduct of the therapy;
- resistance can be understood as a form of communication between the client and the therapist, even to the extent of conceptualizing resistance as a form of supervision;
- resistance can be understood as a particularly fruitful opportunity to work on clinically important issues, such as misunderstandings, managing strong emotions, repairing ruptures in relationships or the client's search to express strong personal commitments.

Resistance as information

Resistance may serve as valuable information about a client's sensitivities, interests and resources. One of Freud's earliest lessons for psychotherapy is the importance of attending to that which is hard to express; the presence of an absence may be significant (Freud 1910; compare A. Freud 1936: 8). A therapist conducting an assessment may notice that the client becomes agitated and hesitant when the therapist asks questions about the client's current workplace and hastily changes the subject; or the client quickly and smoothly provides a brief dismissive answer about a major part of their life, such as their childhood or their current relationships with their partner and children. Of course, there may be many other reasons besides a perceived risk in the therapeutic process for such omissions, apparent hesitations and so on. Hence, resistance in this sense represents a source of tentative hypotheses for further investigation, rather than a definite source of the true situation.

Resistance can also be understood as information about the pattern of the problem, or about ways in which problems are currently managed. A therapist trying to interview a couple about a recent argument may find that their attempts are repeatedly derailed by passionate interruptions from one partner about an apparently unrelated issue, while the other retreats further and further into silence. Although the therapist's original line of inquiry is blocked, the manner in which this occurs might be understood as an enactment in the session of a process which also occurs outside therapy, and is part of a vicious circle which disables intimate conversation between the couple. The degree to which the therapist actually considers this resistance, as opposed to valuable information, may depend on the chronicity with which the pattern replays in therapy and the extent to which it can be further explored or changed, as well as on the therapist's mood and flexibility. If the couple still blocks attempts to explore apparently important issues with the same dynamic in the twentieth session, after the therapist has tried long and hard to share and use the observation therapeutically, the therapist may well feel weary and frustrated and think of the behaviour as unhelpful resistance to be overcome rather than as rich assessment information. Or the therapist may come to see that there are other underlying issues about listening to the other which still need to be explored.

The American hypnotist Milton Erickson (Haley 1985), an inspiration for subsequent developments in neurolinguistic programming, hypnosis and strategic therapy, often approached resistance in this way, not to overcome it but in order to harness the client's characteristic ways of resisting in order to resolve the client's problem. If he observed that the client often set out to prove him wrong about something, then Erickson constructed therapeutic tasks in which the client could either prove him wrong by resolving the problem, or choose to adopt a more cooperative approach for the next stage of the work. A common strategic intervention drawn from this tradition is the therapeutic injunction for resistant clients to 'go slow' with changes, or 'not to try to change at all as you are not ready yet'.

Resistance as feedback

This use of resistance is implicit in some of what we have included above about preventing or overcoming resistance. The therapist may choose to regard resistance as helpful feedback that something in the therapy needs to be done differently. This view of resistance does not necessarily imply that the client is attempting to communicate or guide the therapy, rather that the therapist can gain useful feedback by observing the results of the attempt to intervene or form a therapeutic relationship. If a client seems resistant, perhaps the therapist is using language that is too abstract; or is in conflict with other important commitments in the client's life; or is over-emphasizing the importance of change rather than validating the client's perceptions and feelings (Linehan 1993); or has not sufficiently clarified what the client actually wants. Solution-focused therapy suggests that each client has a unique way of cooperating with a therapist, and apparent resistance should be reframed as feedback for the therapist that they need to find a different way to cooperate with the client, one which will fit better (de Shazer 1984). However, the presence of apparent resistance may not directly specify what is needed other than that it needs to be something different. Within this frame, resistance is reinterpreted as inviting a redirection of therapy, rather than hindering the process.

Resistance as communication

This idea is an elaboration of the notion that resistance can be understood as feedback that something different needs to happen. A therapist may choose to understand apparent resistance as though it were an active attempt by the client to communicate something specific about the direction for a good therapy. (There are some similarities with the psychoanalytic theory discussed in Chapter 4 that projective identification can be understood as an attempt to control the other person; if the therapist experiences resistance, this can be seen as a form of projection by the client.) This way of thinking about resistance is available for therapists who believe that at least some part of the client is actively striving for health and will attempt, even if indirectly or opaquely, to signal what is needed for growth, healing or change (Casement 1985; Langs 1994).

This is compatible with evolutionary theory concerning the adaptive significance of humans as social animals, evolving subtle and sometimes non-verbal ways of communicating needs and eliciting caregiving from others (e.g. Gilbert 2000). From an evolutionary perspective, however, therapists may sometimes tend to interpret attempted communications from others as resistance rather than as helpful guidance because therapists are biased to interpreting communications in terms of their own interests rather than those of the client (Kriegman 2000). In other words, to the extent that the therapist's interests and the client's interests are different, a client's requests for certain interactions and support may be experienced by the therapist as problematic. Therapists' capacity to experience resistance as communication depends in part on the extent to which they are able to place their own needs and desires as secondary to those of the client; and perhaps also to the degree to which they are able to experience a sense of solidarity, kinship and connection with the client (Falicov 1995), thus permitting an empathic stance by acknowledging the client's distress as a matter of shared concern. This idea that resistance can be understood as constructive communication can be a useful antidote to therapists becoming over-attached to one particular way of working. Thinking about the client attempting to act as a supervisor to the therapist can help professionals to remain 'irreverent' (Cecchin *et al.* 1992) towards their most familiar therapeutic constructs.

Resistance as opportunity

Combining the idea of resistance as information about the client's situation with the notion that resistance can be understood as attempted communication with the therapist can be particularly fruitful. Weingarten (1995) uses the term 'cultural resistance' to describe therapeutic work that aims to overturn oppressive and disempowering cultural assumptions and practices which sustain patriarchal and discriminatory societies. Within this frame, resistance to a supposedly therapeutic process can be read as a healthy refusal to adapt meekly to a culture which oppresses the client:

> Resistance in clinical practice has meant obscuring or burying psychological truths or avoiding key memories and feelings, and thus has been seen as an impediment to the creation of a working therapeutic relationship. Resistance is considered a particular challenge in clinical work with adolescent girls, who are known as difficult to treat precisely because of the strength of their resistance and their tendency to leave psychotherapy prematurely. We elaborate the concept of resistance by joining girls' struggle to know what they know and speak about their thoughts and feelings. In doing so we acknowledge the difficulty girls face when their knowledge or feelings seem hurtful to other people or disruptive of relationships. Thus the word 'resistance' takes on new resonances, picking up the notion of healthy resistance, the capacity of the psyche to resist disease processes, and also the concept of political resistance, the willingness to act on one's own knowledge when such action creates trouble. In reframing resistance as a psychological strength, as potentially healthy and

a mark of courage, we draw on the data of our research which show that girls' psychological health in adolescence, like the psychological health of women, depends on their resistance to inauthentic or false relationships.

(Gilligan *et al.* 1991: 1–2)

This implies an intensely communicative value to resistance in psychotherapy, as an attempt to share meaning which is otherwise hard to voice:

I suggest that as clinicians we can develop a growing awareness of how adolescent girls and women try to speak through 'symptoms' and be responsive by acknowledging out loud, in our relationships with them, what cannot be spoken: girls' and women's oppression both in their families and by the culture. In reframing their symptoms as a compromise in an effort to resist this oppression – an attempt to connect to a thwarted desire to be a more authentic person – we can aid the young, sagacious and brave girl of earlier years to emerge.

(Bernardez 1991: 221)

These quotations suggest that resistance can be understood as an expression of preferred values in life, and as an invitation to the therapist to collaborate in pursuing these. Part of the therapist's work might be to support the client to find alternative expressions of this resistance that are less self-injurious (for example, to protest through words rather than self-mutilation). But an equally important task beyond this level is to work with the client to understand, elaborate and pursue their commitments actively and effectively. Of course, the therapist's capacity to respond in this way may be constrained by their agency context. A school counsellor wanting to join with disaffected pupils' resistance to counselling for their 'behaviour problems' as a challenge to oppressive aspects of the curriculum and/or overly rigid hierarchical student–staff relationships may well find herself or himself in direct conflict with senior school staff overseeing disciplinary matters.

From a rather different perspective, psychodynamic therapists are intensely interested in resistance, but have a deeply ambivalent attitude towards it. 'In all cases, analysis of resistance should be the focus of interpretation . . . resistance is often a signpost to change' (Holmes and Bateman 1995: 166). On the one hand, resistance can make therapy fail, but conversely some degree of failure is simultaneously seen as inevitable; and it has great potential value for studying and practising how disappointment can be managed, and for the opportunities failure provides to rehearse the repair of ruptures in the therapeutic relationship (and, by extension, in other important relationships). Resistance in psychoanalysis can be understood as a process of defence against painful meanings and/or painful relationships with others, but a central message of hope in the analytic enterprise is that it is more possible to survive and benefit from painful experiences than the self may initially believe. The point is not that pain and distress should be welcomed for their own sake, but that a therapy which is largely free of resistance lacks opportunities to learn ways to tolerate difficult experience and grow as a result of it.

In forms of analytic work which emphasize difficulties arising from the repression of uncomfortable but important insight into the self and others, some resistance is to be positively welcomed as evidence that the therapist and patient have come within touching distance of important material, which needs to be processed and integrated into the self to achieve a more harmonious balance between different aspects of experience. A therapy that fails to produce or attend to resistance colludes with the patient's experience of anxiety as intolerable or incomprehensible. Resistance should be neither prevented nor overcome, but studied and understood, so that its significance can be appreciated and evaluated in relation to other aspects of self-knowledge. Resistance in therapy constitutes a valuable opportunity to study and revise *in vivo* the kind of defensive procedures that may be used to manage the apparent risks of particular relationships and ways of understanding, and to explore the extent to which those risks are illusory or real, tolerable or intolerable (e.g. Freud 1914; Malan 1976; Judd 1989; compare Winnicott 1975). There are parallels with some cognitive therapy work on trauma, which has rekindled interest in resistance and other 'defensive mental operations' as a potentially valuable indicator of intolerable memories and feelings that may be dissociated and linked with depression and anxiety (Andrews 1995; Brewin 1997).

Analytic work within intersubjective and relational traditions (e.g. Fairburn 1952; Sullivan 1953; Winnicott 1965; Guntrip 1968; Greenberg and Mitchell 1983; Bowlby 1988; Stern 1998; Fonagy 2001; Fonagy *et al.* 2002) places less emphasis on repressed material, and focuses more on the way in which people are object seeking, forming and using relationships with others to generate and revise experience and self. Such traditions are concerned with the complex interactions between the external world of a patient's relationships with others and the inner world of the patient, with the different aspects of the self in relation to one another and to introjected models or representations of other persons (Mitchell and Black (1995) and Holmes and Bateman (1995) provide helpful maps to locate this work in relation to other analytic arguments). Within such approaches, the phenomena of failure and resistance within the therapeutic process have a crucial positive function, as an arena in which the possibilities for making, breaking and repairing relational connections with another (the therapist) can be explored, understood and experimented with. New possibilities for entering into and maintaining relationships with others, and with previously marginalized or disowned aspects of self, can be evolved and practised.

Attachment-based and cognitive-analytic therapies incorporate these themes in contemporary integrative approaches (e.g. Ryle 1997; Holmes 2001). Some recent developments in cognitive therapy also place an emphasis on resistance between client and therapist as an opportunity to understand and change processes of relationship rupture and repair (Safran and Segal 1990; Young 1994).

Therapists who are too organized around the idea of having a warm and collaborative working alliance with their clients may deny them important living and immediate opportunities for developing new ways of addressing difficulties in relationships, including powerful but supposedly negative feelings and responses to failures (Winnicott 1975). Representing a Winnicottian view, Jacobs writes:

> A corrective experience is never enough, and it is the failures, 'often quite small ones', that enable the patient to hate the therapist, and to bring the original environmental failures into the transference. The survival of the therapist . . . is as important in therapy as the survival of the parent in child and adolescent development. Even if 'in the end we succeed by failing' (Winnicott 1965: 258), this is again similar to what Winnicott says is inevitable in parenting. It does in fact provide a rather different example of a corrective experience, because this time, for some reason we can never be sure of, our failure succeeds in helping the patient develop.
>
> (Jacobs 1995: 61)

Conclusion

In this chapter we have described resistance as a particular subform of defences arising within the therapeutic encounter itself. We describe how therapies may theorize resistance differently, and indeed may locate resistance in different ways. An important element of our understanding of resistance is its perspectival nature. Resistance differs according to the perspective of person or agency experiencing the phenomenon; and this in turn is influenced by prevailing differential relationships of power, where the powerful have the capacity to affect the attribution of meaning to the experience of resistance by all participants. We have also described some attitudes or technical postures which therapists may adopt towards resistance, which can broadly be categorized as minimizing, overcoming or utilizing resistance. In the next chapter, we extend some of these arguments into a consideration of defensive themes outside the consulting room, into the wider domain of psychotherapy training, supervision and other aspects of professionalism.

Defensive concepts and professionalism

Introduction

We have included throughout our text references to the employment of defences in situations beyond the one-to-one therapeutic relationship: to defences in everyday life, as well as the defensiveness engendered in families, groups and organizations. In this final chapter we particularly reflect on some defensive issues in relation to organizational and professional processes. After some general considerations concerning defences and organizations, we focus on:

- defences and initial training in therapy;
- clinical supervision, defences and resistance;
- evidence-based practice;
- professionalism.

We conclude by making the bold suggestion that the enterprise of psychotherapy and counselling as a whole can be understood as a form of defence for society.

We recognize that some therapists, following their training, have little or no contact with organizational settings and professional institutions, working alone in private practice with clients who have self-referred. In some countries, such as Britain, there is currently no statutory requirement for individual psychotherapists to have undertaken any specific form of professional training, and no requirement for clinical supervision or continuing professional development. However, in practice most therapists have current and historic relationships with a range of professional organizations or networks, which may themselves have complex interconnections. Such organizations include:

- training institutions which organize therapists' initial trainings and/or continuing professional development programmes;
- national and international bodies which offer accreditation or registration for therapists and counsellors, alongside processes for responding to complaints and allegations of misconduct and malpractice;
- organizations which employ, contract with or at least regularly refer clients to therapists and counsellors;
- training institutions in which the therapist provides teaching, clinical supervision and/or trainee placements, and/or examining and accreditation reviews;
- national bodies which publish and promote quality standards and requirements or guidelines for psychotherapeutic practice.

Defences may operate within and between these organizational contexts to mediate against apparent threats. An organization may itself be perceived as generating a potential threat, as experienced by individuals and external groups. For example, the activities of a new government body established to promote national guidelines for psychotherapy with children are likely to be regarded with some trepidation by therapists working in child and adolescent mental health, even by those clinicians who, in principle at least, are already in favour of coordinated national policy development.

Conversely, organizations may experience themselves as threatened by external sources and respond defensively. A psychotherapy service may feel under pressure to change practice to include more routine outcome evaluation if it learns that this will be a focus for an inspection by a commissioning body. Alternatively, the same service might explore ways to divert or delay the inspection, or prepare a documentary 'smokescreen' simulating compliance but without making substantial changes in practice. Within the United States, many managed health care organizations routinely require a diagnostic categorization of the client in order to authorize payment to the therapist, meaning that psychotherapists must resort to diagnosis to protect their income streams, whether or not this is consistent with their clinical epistemology (Hoyt 1995).

Some institutions form as a collective defensive response to dangers experienced by individuals in the therapeutic arena. This might be seen as one of the motives for Freud's inner circle of disciples, each given a ring, to defend 'the Cause' (Clark 1980). Similarly, support networks formed by psychotherapy trainees outside their formal course structure can be read as having a defensive function. Some survivors of abuse from therapists have formed networks to support each other and campaign for more respectful and non-abusive practice, attempting to influence other organizations within the psychotherapy arena, such as the training and accrediting bodies.

Institutions exercising defensive functions may in turn be experienced by others as constituting a threat. Psychotherapists who are unused to accounting for their practice to other professions or to non-professionals may feel challenged if their employer invites a mental health user or psychotherapy survivor organization to audit clinical practice in their workplace. Psychotherapists working within, for instance, a humanistic model may feel intimidated by well organized and powerful learned societies, operating to protect and advance the interests of cognitive-behavioural therapists, psychoanalytic workers or psychologists specializing in psychotherapy or counselling.

Organizational processes may also be experienced by members within an institution as presenting risks which need to be defended against, while organizations themselves may feel threatened from within by dissidents and rebels. Perceived threats may be 'top-down' (for example, when senior managers unilaterally introduce a new policy limiting the number of sessions that can be offered to a client, or when training course directors introduce additional assessment requirements), or 'bottom-up' (for example, when supervisees challenge the authority and competence of their supervisor directly or indirectly). Organizational subsystems may also pose risks to one another laterally: for example, if two clinics offering different types of psychotherapy within the same overall service appear to compete for resources and status, or attempt to contain their respective workloads by referring across to the other clinic.

The complex and often Protean nature of psychotherapeutic work presents particular dilemmas to the management of risk within therapy-related organizations, which have implications for training, clinical supervision and quality assurance processes, such as an emphasis on evidence-based practice. On the one hand, from a 'top-down' consensus managerial perspective (see Collins 2002) some risks relating to uncertainty can be reduced by limiting the delegation of decision-making power down an organizational hierarchy, and mandating detailed monitoring and reporting processes from the bottom up (for example, instructing clinical supervisors to take an explicit case management and audit role). The regulation of, or response to, decision-making within an organization can be seen as a defensive strategy.

On the other hand, this kind of detailed hierarchical control is likely to: (a) increase the perception of threat by subordinates – so inciting resistance – as their apparent autonomy and sense of self-regard is compromised; (b) undermine any culture of trust within the organization; and (c) limit the capacity of 'lower-level' workers (therapists, supervisors, trainees) to respond flexibly and meaningfully to the specifics of the actual clinical situation they are faced with. In managerial jargon, autonomous self-organizing units of a horizontally decentralized organization can develop their potential for flexibility only to the extent that decision-making is delegated to them (Weick 1982). A low level of delegation in decision-making may be functional and least likely to compromise organizational functioning in situations where there are relatively few uncertainties, and where flexibility, discretion and responsiveness to local conditions are not a requirement. Such circumstances are, however, extremely rare in the psychotherapeutic domain, where it is necessary to emphasize the 'responsible work' (Volberda 1999) of clinicians who have both constructive capabilities and needs of their own. While this would be important in any organizational field dealing with complex and changing phenomena, psychotherapy is intimately concerned with the constructive engagement of the therapist and client's sense and use of self. Consequently, any effective psychotherapy service or training course must find ways to trust their employees or trainees to be themselves. Processes which endanger the culture of trust are particularly corrosive to psychotherapy organizations.

Although the benefits of effective delegation within complex organizations are generally accepted, from a senior management perspective this entails a degree of risk. Coordination among activities can be difficult to ensure. Individuals and groups that constitute work units are of course active in construing their context, and in practice may not interpret the organization's shared purpose in the same way as managers/seniors, even where there is apparent agreement at the level of rhetoric. Senior management (such as service heads or directors of therapy training) balance the potential payoff of delegation or the enabling of subordinates to author truth against the risk of lack of shared vision and poor coordination. The effects of subordinates' reinterpretation of goals and tasks are often described in terms of vested interests in lower hierarchical levels, which in turn are seen as breeding resistance to organizational change, and as such a source of organizational vulnerability. If there is an assumption of a unidirectional monopoly on truth from the top down, this pathologizes challenges by subordinates in the same way that a client's or patient's dispute regarding the psychotherapy process may be dismissed or interpreted as evidence of pathology, or worse still as a failure to commit to or engage in the psychotherapy process. In both contexts if the power wielders are to exploit the potential of knowledge and insights available from the client or employee they must be sufficiently robust to hear what they have to say.

Collaborative meaning-making in organizations that transcends working groups and hierarchical demarcation is described as 'participation' by functionalist organizational theorists (Collins 2002). Participation is seen as the most effective strategy to ensure integration and to offset the threat posed by delegation (Khandwalla 1977). In participative organizations subordinates can give opinions, make suggestions and present arguments. Superiors, however, always make the final decision. Participation is seen in organizational theory as enhancing the self-initiative and responsibility of subordinates. Low levels of participation increase the risks of poor quality decision-making as a consequence of reduced levels of information sharing. Volberda (1999) argues that low levels of participation foster segmentalism within organizations and lead inevitably to inadequate responses to non-routine problem-solving, which actually benefits from multiple perspectives. A high degree of participation is seen as enhancing global, richer and more integrated decisions, based on various contributions of lower levels. Moreover, participation is seen as helping different levels of the organization to develop the capacity to think about the broader goals, with the implication that there will be enhanced commitment in the implementation of decisions (French and Bell 1999).

However, organizational theories examining resistance to change from a top-down perspective may not sufficiently encompass the range of different purposes and agendas being pursued by participants in therapeutic organizations and interactions (Campbell 2000). Although the interests of therapist and client, supervisor and supervisee, trainer and trainee, therapy commissioner and therapy provider overlap to some degree, they may also be divergent. Failing to acknowledge this may operate as a short-term defence against anxieties concerning conflict, but in the medium and longer term is likely to be counter-productive, since participants will find themselves working at cross-purposes, but unable to discuss this and negotiate compromises.

Initial training in therapy

There are many disparate influences acting upon stakeholders involved in the process of professional training in therapy. Professional bodies of accreditation and registration, training institutions, trainers, employers, supervisors and trainees generally cooperate, but sometimes they clash with each other as they pursue their own unique set of objectives and priorities. From the outset, there are substantial barriers to psychotherapy training in many institutions relating to fees, time commitment and requirements for prior academic qualifications. Each of these might differentially disadvantage applicants from particular community sectors, such as women, working-class people, would-be therapists from ethnic minority groups and so on. The barriers potentially involved are not simply restricted to the material factors such as time and money, but may also relate to the anti-discriminatory ethos and lack of flexibility of the trainers and the host institution. Barriers may be covert, as with the discriminatory effect of providing a psychotherapy course with an inflexible structure for attendance with no child care facilities, or they may be overt. A longstanding case in point has been the institutionalized reluctance of psychoanalytic training institutions to pass candidate analysts who maintain a gay or lesbian identity following their training analysis (Cunningham 1991; compare Frosh 1997).

Once training has begun, defensive concepts are often invoked in theorizing the interface between trainee and training provider. Trainees and their clients are the least powerful stakeholders in the training enterprise. They are the least likely to have an authoritative voice in defining or setting standards. They seek privileged knowledge. They are assessed. Trainees need to seek leave to practise, while their clients seek access to services that will ease distress. Although trainers certainly stand to gain in reputation and future applications by passing successful candidates, trainers also act as a defence for the profession and for the trainee's potential future clients, by gatekeeping against would-be therapists who are not fit to practise. Trainers may also aim to defend an established 'tradition' or culture in their school of psychotherapy or counselling, where questioning of traditional views can even lead to the status of 'heretic'. Trainers and supervisors may also seek to defend and preserve their personal high status, as senior practitioners fit to train and accredit others.

Trainers are versed in the institutional aims and objectives of training. They have a course mapped out. They are likely to be authors of their particular course and have had sufficient experience in it to internalize it. By contrast, even trainees who appear to share an enthusiastic initial commitment to the values of any given training may find themselves surprised and/or disappointed over time as they come to appreciate the reality and substance of its implementation. As a result of the trainee's engagement in an established programme of training they are precluded from the opportunity to co-create or negotiate their rite of passage. Questions raised by trainees about why training takes the form it does are likely to be interpreted as evidence of defensiveness and resistance rather than a constructive encounter where new, shared meanings may evolve.

This institutionalized tendency to close ranks and defend the status quo is paradoxically amplified by the trainer/trainee role relationship. Trainers have a knowledge status that exceeds that of the trainee in the domain that they seek to train, which is as it should be if they are to discharge their responsibility legitimately. This status requirement has a tendency to generalize to the extent that the trainer resists any threat to sharing power. The negotiation of meaning in a collaborative way can undermine traditional power relationships. In order to maintain an identity as a 'good teacher' the trainer may feel incited to truncate communication in a bid to retain their status as authoritative. This pressure may feel particularly marked for trainers who are working with trainee therapists who already have substantial life experience, successful prior histories in other helping professions and previous training in another model of psychotherapy or counselling. However, in this process the personal capacities and self-reflexivity of the trainee can become marginalized, which is likely to impact adversely on their therapeutic work with clients. Psychotherapy trainers face the paradoxical task of providing trainees with 'freedom to learn' (Rogers 1969) and being themselves congruently and spontaneously with their clients, while paradoxically taking on the responsibility of encouraging the trainee to become somewhat different from what they were at the outset. There may also be significant variations between trainers concerning the degree to which they themselves anticipate and welcome the prospect of being further transformed themselves through their work with many trainees over the years. These dilemmas can be concealed to some degree by presenting psychotherapy and counselling as a technical process involving expert skills and techniques (see the companion volume in this series, Rowan and Jacobs 2002: Chapter 2), yet they are increasingly apparent in psychotherapy trainings which emphasize the importance of the therapeutic relationship and self-reflexivity.

Trainers may be particularly disposed to invoke defensive responses in relation to trainees through a blurring of the boundaries between participating in practice and teaching. Training programmes, designed by trainers and influenced by accreditation bodies, often require trainees to become clients as a rite of passage, on the assumption that pathological defences must be exorcised or converted into more functional ones (Davy 2002b). Indeed, the potentially subversive action of questioning the expensive and time-consuming need for personal therapy in training may be interpreted by trainers as evidence of defensiveness and resistance. However, the role of the personal therapist in defending the profession and clients against trainees who are psychologically unsuited to practise as psychotherapists is very weak. This is partly because there is no good evidence base to suggest that personal therapists can make accurate judgements of this kind anyway, and partly because a conflict arises between the defence of the profession and protecting the confidentiality of the trainees' own therapy. Personal therapists are not generally expected to report on the candidate's suitability to become a psychotherapist or counsellor.

Defensive discourses also operate between training institutions and their relevant bodies of accreditation. Given the power imbalance involved, interpretation of the actions of the less powerful are subject to suspicion where they are not consistent with the directives of the more powerful. The reputation and authority of each institutional stakeholder is tested in encounters where meanings are in conflict. A dynamic common to institutional tension is that each participant requires a degree of power and authority to function, and thus any challenge to this threatens the viability of each party to deliver and ultimately survive in their role. From a personal construct perspective this propensity to over-estimate the threat imbued in particular events can be understood in terms of the invalidation of core constructs. Core constructs are concerned with the maintenance of identity and, from an individual psychological perspective, with the continuity of self (Mahoney 1991; Fransella 2003). Thus, although the challenge may be at a low level of significance in terms of how it may be perceived by others, it is what the event signifies that is central to the experience of threat. Resistance in this sense can be seen as a strategy for retaining integrity.

Tensions inevitably exist within therapy training institutions. Commercial pressure to maximize efficiency can be met with resistance from academics who interpret this push as a distraction from delivering training of the highest quality. Academics' resistance to cost-cutting initiatives can be interpreted as a failure to grasp the significance of the pressure and constraints that the institution operates within. In turn, academics' interpretation of the failure of the institution to be forthcoming with resources can be read as a failure of the executive to understand the nature and significance of the task that is undertaken in the pursuit of educational service delivery. Serving as a barrier to common understanding is the demarcation of roles and the concentration of specific objectives within work units within the organizational structure. This circumstance is particularly ironic given that academics with often-limited training in management occupy executive roles. In much of the business world, specifically trained managers make management decisions and leave product specialists to develop and deliver the product. In a situation where groups could have much in common they are pitted against one another through role specialization, and distinct and distancing priorities.

Clinical supervision

Researching the multiple functions of clinical supervision, Carroll (1996) notes that most definitions of supervision involve overseeing and evaluating therapeutic practice. This explicitly privileges the sight of the observer-supervisor and therefore establishes their authority in authoring the process. However, Carroll also finds that many supervisors tend to be least comfortable with these evaluative, summative and directorial aspects of their role, preferring the supportive, educational and formative work involved in supervision.

This assessment function of supervision is most evident in training contexts where the clinical supervisor's report directly affects the trainee's progression. However, clinical supervision for qualified therapists and counsellors is also often presented as a key means to ensure good quality practice. Clinical supervision within a discourse of professionalism may be viewed as a means to promote organizational standards directly, through monitoring case work and synchronizing team efforts, or more subtly as a form of 'dressage' (Foucault 1984). Supervision trains staff to watch and monitor themselves continuously in comparison with organizational aims and culture, through the installation of an 'internal supervisor' (Casement 1985, 1990). Clinical supervision in this sense constitutes a form of professional or personal governance (i.e. self-management and discipline), which could be likened to Foucault's (1977) theorization of the confessional as a means to encourage persons to monitor and control themselves with ever-greater self-discipline. This is a more insidious and economical form of power than direct observation and control by others.

The multiple functions of the roles of the key players in clinical supervision can operate to promote a defensiveness and resistance that serves to keep therapist and supervisor apart at a safe distance which is insufficiently challenging or authentic. Supervisees want to be supported and may need a source of new ideas and a sounding board, but also simultaneously feel threatened by the prospect of exposing failures, doubts and problems (Ladany *et al.* 1996; Webb and Wheeler 1998; Webb 2000; compare White 2002). Support and assessment are both explicit functions of supervision, particularly in training contexts, and conflict can arise in the discharge of these responsibilities. Supervisees are encouraged to disclose in a context where disclosure may identify poor performance. Poor performance invalidates their striving to be an accomplished therapist or therapist in training. Where vocation is strongly linked to identity, the threat to self is increased. Thus the therapist who works hardest to achieve mastery is at greatest risk of invalidation and arguably most resistant to feedback from the supervisor. In turn, supervisors who find themselves with little to say may develop anxiety related to incompetence. The presentation of neat and tidy stories of clinical work by supervisees can leave the supervisor floundering and unable to add value to their narrative. This complex dynamic can give rise to threat and tension, which may in turn promote defensive posturing where collaboration, transparency and shared meaning-making become compromised.

For example, it is not uncommon for supervisors to feel that a trainee is being 'resistant', 'non-compliant' or 'over-defended' in some way against adequate reflection on their work or some necessary personal development. When clinical supervision is conceptualized as a form of psychotherapeutic interaction (rather than as, for example, education, problem-solving or skills practice and rehearsal), supervisees may experience themselves as mainly needing to improve their interpersonal skills and interpret or resolve intrapsychic conflicts which may be countertransferentially linked with their clinical practice. Within a psychotherapeutic discourse, supervisors may experience discomfort if supervisees claim to be functioning well, analogous to the problems therapists may face in engaging mandated clients.

Equally, it appears that many trainees experience their supervisors as threatening or even downright abusive (Kaberry 2000) and feel a need to adopt defensive positions such as highly selective case presentation. Supervisors may themselves feel under pressure to pre-serve and project an image of competency and maturity, and resort to a variety of potentially counter-productive defensive stances to underpin this, including hiding behind theory and self-deception about the degree to which they understand a complex and difficult interaction with their supervisee. Although these dynamics may be particularly acute in trainer–trainee relationships because of the com-bination of stark power differentials, requirements in training for intensive supervision and developmental dilemmas of professional self-esteem and identity, 'conscious incompetence' and so on, it seems likely that experienced therapists and their supervisors or con-sultants may experience similar pressures and dilemmas. These issues are also likely to be exacerbated where the clinical material which needs to be considered is particularly confused, demanding or secondarily traumatizing for the therapist, and where dimensions of difference between supervisor, supervisee and client, such as those of culture and gender, are insufficiently understood or attended to (e.g. Cox 1996; Down *et al.* 2000; Haines 2000).

Clinical supervision is often justified as a defence for clients against ineffective or unethical practice. However, there is actually little evi-dence that clinical supervision changes practitioner behaviour to produce beneficial effects on clinical outcomes for clients/patients, or actually protects clients from abuse by practitioners (Davy 2002a). Most research on the effects of supervision focuses on behaviours and attitudes within supervision and the perceptions of supervisees and/ or supervisors on the supervisory relationship and roles, rather than actual effects experienced by clients. There is some evidence that trainees with positive supervisory relationships also tend to have positive therapeutic relationships with clients (Patton and Kivlighan 1997), but such correlational studies do not demonstrate causal connections.

Much supervision is conducted through retrospective verbal accounts of practice by a therapist to a supervisor who was not present for the session between therapist and client. Under these circum-stances the therapist is the only source of information for the super-visor. There is a parallel between the widespread adoption of clinical supervision focusing on the supervisee's 'phantasy of the client' meeting the supervisor's 'phantasy of the client' (Jacobs 1996), and Freud's renunciation of the material truths motivating his patients' descriptions of abuse (Masson 1985a). Without a focus on actual client outcomes, clinical supervision as personal governance or self-surveillance has questionable value for ensuring public accountability, although it may be valuable for motivating and supporting therapists, and provide them with opportunities for learning and reflection which some, but not all, will use well. It may be that clinical supervision is more valuable as a defence for therapists against stress resulting from their work and clients' reactions than as a defence for clients against poor therapy (Yegdich 1999).

The emphasis on clinical supervision as a primary means for ensuring quality services may reflect a situation in which clinical supervision is provided and promoted by some professionals because they can offer it and because they believe they will profit from this as supervisors, rather than because it meets an identified consumer need or demand. It could be argued that clinical supervision provides a rhetorical mechanism (as quality assurance) in both professional and managerial discourse to forestall demands for more direct accountability to users, which would be inherent in a consumerist discourse. An important way to distinguish this conservative professional defence from other more positive purposes for clinical supervision is to examine in any given setting whether clinical supervision is just one means among many, such as evidence-based practice, to promote quality services and reflect on feedback from clients, or whether it is the only substantial arena in which the largely private work of therapy is reviewed.

Evidence-based practice

> In the past – and perhaps still at present – quite a number of clinicians and institutions have developed their own brand of psychotherapy and prescribed this without evaluating the benefits to a particular patient. Here patients have to fit the treatment and if they do not respond, they risk the 'diagnosis' of 'treatment resistance'. The alternative 'diagnosis', namely that the treatment was 'patient resistant', not fitting the patient's individual needs and requirements, is hardly ever made. One of the more positive aspects of the new fetish of evidence-based medicine (Sackett *et al.* 1996) is the implied emphasis on matching appropriate treatments to patients (and their conditions) and not the other way round!
>
> (Asen 2002, 55–56)

Many therapists work in contexts where there are increasing demands by managers, funding agencies and others that therapeutic approaches are justified and evaluated. One manifestation of this is the increasing prominence of the construct of evidence-based practice (Mace *et al.* 2001). Psychotherapists and counsellors wanting to retain public funding may feel under pressure to produce confident declarations of knowledge and effectiveness. As with clinical supervision, moves to promote evidence-based practice in psychotherapy can be read as a well intentioned attempt to improve the quality of therapy services and to protect clients from poor practice, as Asen's remarks suggest, but also as a defensive strategy to protect resources for psychotherapy.

In an increasingly competitive therapy market place, combined with some apparent trends towards user empowerment and democratization of the helping professions, different psychotherapy and counselling schools or training institutions may also become defensive about their prospects and position in relation to other therapies (e.g. Crane and Hafen 2002). A school of therapy which fails to research and publish an evidence base acceptable to funders is likely to lose out relative to competitor organizations whose therapists can claim evidential backing that appeals to those who control the purse strings.

The psychotherapies vary greatly in their emphasis on providing empirical foundations for their theoretical superstructures. In part this reflects the different historical traditions, skills and opportunities available to therapists from different schools. For example, many cognitive-behavioural therapists come from disciplinary bases such as psychology, which has a dominant tradition over the past century of privileging positivist empiricism, whereas many early psychoanalysts were doctors with a strong interest in case lore and clinical observation. However, this also reflects widely divergent views about the clinical importance and the epistemological validity of theory–practice relationships. In turn this reflects the relative importance of theoretical foundations versus empirical and clinical 'evidence', and related arguments about which kinds of evidence are genuinely meaningful in developing evidence-based practice, and its neglected twin, practice-based evidence.

Although evidence-based practice can be understood as a means to defend clients from poor therapy, and for psychotherapies to protect resources for their work, evidence-based practice can itself become a source of threat for therapists and so provoke resistance or defensive operations. As already suggested, some schools of therapy may feel under pressure to protect their position by catching up with others with a stronger tradition of empirical research. At a more personal level, each therapist has contextual frames for the self-appraisal of their professional practice. Cumulative implicative challenges from an emerging evidence base that overturn these risk undermining a therapist's sense of professional identity and competence ('Have I been letting my clients down by providing ineffective therapy all these years?'). Wessely (2001) argues that one of the principal values of a well designed randomized controlled trial is its capacity to disprove cherished assumptions. This is also its risk for a therapist's sense of personal meaning (Bugental and Bugental 1984; Liotti 1989; Rogers 1989; Spinelli 2001).

Mason has argued (1993) that therapy needs conditions of 'safe uncertainty' in which risks and ambiguities can be both tolerated and explored, allowing new understanding and action. This echoes older psychotherapeutic traditions concerned with the dual significance of containment, empathy and warmth, combined with unknowing and challenge. This construction of therapy suggests that an excessive commitment to conduct therapy in a particular way (by client, therapist, supervisor or manager) can be understood as a potentially counter-therapeutic attempt to reduce the anxiety of uncertainty through 'safe certainty'. Evidence-based practice can be viewed as a way of increasing either safety in a session or the degree of certainty. If therapists draw on evidence to promote a sense of safety then it may be helpful, but not if this use of evidence closes down options for reviewing and revising meanings by prematurely foreclosing certainty.

This implies that therapists need to attend carefully to the way in which they use the evidence base to inform their therapy. However, a more complex issue concerns the way in which power inheres in the capacity to define the rules of evidence, determining the admissibility and weighting of evidence. Who gets to decide what counts as evidence, which questions are asked and how different kinds of evidence are to be compared? Typically, influential hierarchies of evidence place large-scale professional studies such as randomized control trials as the 'gold standard', while user perspectives and phenomenological accounts are given very little weight in comparison.

It is open to question how much evidence-based practice shapes rather than justifies practice. This issue is murky partly because many evidential 'gamekeepers' (e.g. journal editors and reviewers) were or are also 'poachers'. Papers examining the efficacy of psychological therapies are reviewed by psychological therapists (often from the same discipline or orientation), and then summarized by psychological therapists working for official bodies. It is difficult to disentangle how 'external' evidence really is, given the vested interests and prior theoretical commitments (Sturdee 2001) of those who own the means of evidential production, distribution and exchange.

This analysis suggests a potential opposition between evidence-based practice and 'user involvement' in the development of psycho-therapy services. Although users are to be asked for their views, the agenda for consultation is shaped primarily by professional evidence bases. Adapting Henry Ford, clients can seek 'any colour therapy they like', as long as it is evidence-based according to the professionals' criteria! This view of evidence-based practice suggests a function of preserving professional status and power in the face of emerging demands for consumer choice and client empowerment. Evidence-based practice also operates partly to underpin therapy's claims to professionalization. However, as Mowbray (1995) and others have argued, the advantages of professionalism for health care patients or therapy clients are debatable (Menzies-Lyth 1960; Illich 1975; Rogers 1991; House 2003).

If a dominant version of evidence-based practice marginalizes certain kinds of problem, this may contribute to the suppression of debate and recognition of the difficulty. This will perhaps make it hard to obtain treatment or redress for a problem which is not officially recognized; or more pervasively make it difficult to speak of or even think about certain kinds of problem meaningfully. The predominant organization of evidence-based practice around individual diagnosis rather than formulation/hypothesis tends to reproduce intrapsychic understandings of distress, rather than relational ones, and might serve to obscure socio-cultural and economic factors. Much client distress seems well accounted for by poverty, poor housing, unemployment, violence, alcohol misuse, abuse, racism and other forms of discrimination, enforced migration and serious illness (see also the critique of psychopathologies in the companion volume in this series, Bhugra and Davies 2003). Clinically, it would seem as plausible to produce guides to the evidence base for psychotherapists organized around titles such as 'Violence', 'Racism', 'Poor housing', 'Unmet educational needs', 'Survivor's guide to psychotherapy and medication', 'Feminist guide to eating distress' and so on.

Conversely, as Bhugra and Davies (2003) make plain, the existence of an institutionally sanctioned evidence base about a particular problem such as 'personality disorder' helps to create its pathological reality. In the twentieth century, arguments about effective ways to treat homosexuality presupposed and then reproduced the idea that being gay or lesbian was problematic (Kutchins and Kirk 1999).

Evidence-based practice helps to construct and reproduce therapeutic practice rather than simply describe it.

All such categorizations direct attention away from evidence about the therapist's self. Whatever external evidence has to offer, its selection and application is mediated through the person of the therapist. For clients as consumers, a valuable evidence-based guide could be organized around evaluations of individually named therapists, rather than models and problems. However, it is not difficult to imagine how threatening this prospect might seem to many psychotherapists, who might defensively prefer to emphasize their adherence to a particular brand-name therapy rather than publicize their personal qualities, personal outcome data and positive and negative client testimonials. None the less, we suggest that therapists concerned with self-reflexivity should attempt to research an intimately proximal evidence base about themselves (Flaskas and Perlesz 1996; Hildebrand 1998), and consider which aspects could and should be shared with clients.

Professionalism

As the preceding sections on clinical supervision and evidence-based practice suggest, there are potential ambiguities within psychotherapy about the defensive functions of professionalism and related developments, such as accreditation standards, registration, complaints procedures and requirements for continuing professional development for re-registration.

These are often presented as structures and processes which are intended to defend the public from bad therapy or bad therapists. For instance, a client who feels they have been exploited or abused by their therapist may be able to seek redress and protect future clients by complaining to that therapist's professional registration body. That body may already have helped to construct some defences against abusive practice by publishing information for the public about ethical psychotherapy, and perhaps by mandating some focus on ethical practice and on detecting professional abuses in psychotherapy and counselling trainings.

How effective this action is will of course depend on many factors, including the degree to which non-therapists are powerful within the complaints process, and the scope for abusive therapists to continue practising even if expelled from their professional body. At the time of writing, there is no statutory requirement for a therapist to belong to any professional body or register in Britain, so that even a therapist barred from all professional organizations is still able to offer psychotherapy services to the public. To this extent, the establishment of professional bodies and complaints proceedings may partly represent a comforting illusion of defence against abusive practice rather than a genuinely effective measure. The history of psychotherapy also has many examples of psychotherapists well regarded in their profession who have abused their clients (Masson 1993), so clients and colleagues clearly cannot assume that a therapist is safe simply because he or she appears professional and has brilliant credentials.

Although the development of professionalization in a discipline such as therapy is usually presented and justified in terms of proposed benefits for service users, such as harmonization of training standards and rigour in complaints handling, it is also possible to understand moves towards professionalism as a defensive strategy, protecting the interests of the providers of therapy from possible competitors, or from detailed scrutiny by users and funders of therapy. As George Bernard Shaw argued, professions can operate as conspiracies against the laity.

Professionalization implies an increase in status and recognition, and the development of important roles which are not open to those outside the profession. Professionals are also expected to review the quality of their own actions and skills, a form of personal accountability. Historically, this has also been associated with a kind of closed shop. Moves to enhance therapy training standards through longer and more rigorous courses, or additional personal therapy and supervision requirements, can sometimes be interpreted, at least in part, as steps by those already qualified as therapists to consolidate their powerful position at the top of the professional tree. Professions reserve certain roles and tasks for themselves, but also set the standards by which they should be judged, denying that outsiders are competent to make such evaluations (Larson 1977). Traditionally, professional loyalty is primarily to fellow professionals, not to other organizations and management.

Benefit for clients is claimed, but the advantages of professionalism for the public are debatable (Menzies-Lyth 1960; Illich 1975; Rogers 1991; Mowbray 1995; House 2003). For example, creeping professionalism may render ordinary human experience, such as bereavement and loss, mysterious and esoteric as expert knowledge is constructed. This has the potential to divorce people from important non-professional support systems, shaking their faith in their own personal understanding and means of self-healing (Walter 2000).

Greater professionalization of therapy services may present a barrier for those clients who would prefer more access to informal, democratic services with substantial input from lay workers and fellow users. Professionalism may also incite some clinicians to adopt a particular facade, to play the part, which may distance that therapist from their own personal feelings and experience, and inhibit empathy with clients in distress. This professional facade can become an important but counter-therapeutic defensive mechanism for therapists, especially where it is so overused that it becomes habitual.

Unlike some of these authors cited above, we are not seeking to argue that professionalism in psychotherapy and the helping professions is wrong *per se*. Instead, we suggest that therapists should adopt a constructively self-critical stance when they notice themselves justifying arguments for higher status, more training, pay increases and so on solely in terms of clients' best interests. They should also allow themselves to notice instances where professionalism is used defensively to distance the therapist from their clients rather than to increase empathic connection and shared inquiry. Our ingenuity in finding ways to protect ourselves from the sadness and pain inherent in clinical practice knows no bounds.

Psychotherapy as a societal defence

The very existence of psychotherapy and counselling, and other helping professions concerned with mental health and illness, can be understood as a kind of defensive process protecting the interests and self-images of those not labelled deviant or in need of help (Szasz 1961; Foucault 1965; Ussher 1991; Parker *et al.* 1995). It also ensnares those deemed mentally healthy in the straitjacketed ways of being required to avoid being seen as mentally unwell. The Western world was intensely critical of abuses within the mental health system of the communist bloc, used to invalidate political and social dissent. However, it is not itself immune from such dynamics, as the British suffragettes found in the early twentieth century when they pushed for women's civil rights and were criticized or even imprisoned as mad; or as many gay people found in the twentieth century when therapists sought to 'cure' them of their 'illness' (Kitzinger and Perkins 1993; Kutchins and Kirk 1999).

The relationship between therapies and the broader social context is complex and ambivalent (Pilgrim 1997). Smail (e.g. 1996) has argued against professionalized therapy as a poor palliative for taking care of one another in the real, everyday community through pro-gressive political and personal practice and responsibility. However, as with Masson's criticism of therapy, it is debatable how much this reflects a personal polemic rather than a balanced appraisal of the mixed evidence around the value and effectiveness of therapy (Pilgrim 1992; Owen 1995). On the one hand, the recognition and treatment of eating disorders as a kind of personal distress amenable to therapy may have helped to raise awareness of societal pressures, particularly (though not exclusively) on women, regarding themes such as body image and sexuality. On the other hand, psycho-therapeutic theories about eating problems may also deflect critical attention and resources away from efforts to challenge and reform cultural discourses around diet, gender, sexuality etc. and the exploit-ative corporate practices of food, fashion, advertising and pharma-ceutical multinationals. The development of psychotherapy for patients with anorexia still places responsibility for change primarily with the anorexic people and their families, not with the media and global capitalism.

Psychotherapeutic theory and institutions can sometimes be recruited as a defence for an established but threatened social order. Discussing the mixed blessings of Winnicott's psychotherapeutic theories for women, Pilgrim writes that Winnicott 'was an ambiguous hero. In charging mothers with the biological duty to offer "good-enough" care for their infants, he began a post-war trend in welfare professional surveillance . . . Such a professional preoccupation with mothering skills has often been an oppressive burden upon young women who are already struggling with depression and material dis-advantage' (Pilgrim 1997: 132). Similar charges have been made against Bowlby's development of attachment theory, which has richly influenced many contemporary forms of psychotherapy (e.g. Cassidy and Shaver 1999; Fonagy 2001; Holmes 2001). On the one hand Bowlby's work highlighted the enormous value, importance and subtlety of mothering to children's long-term development; on the other his theories served a significant defensive function for patri-archy in helping to re-establish and preserve male domination in the workplace as men returned to the labour force after military service in the Second World War.

Masson (1985a) has argued that Freud's abandonment of the seduc-tion hypothesis constituted a formidable barrier for many years bias-ing his followers against believing clients' stories of terrible abuse, because Freud's subsequent emphasis on fantasy and intrapsychic functioning led accounts of real events to be treated as coded 'metaphoric' messages about the nature of the clients' unconscious mind. Arguably, similar defensive dynamics operate in relation to child abuse, with the establishment of specialist therapeutic teams operating to provide skilled specialist services to children in dire need, but also to collude in a collective defence against the high frequency of child abuse that could be noticed and treated in non-specialist clinics. There is some parallel between the professional development of such specialist services and specialist theories about the nature of child abuse and its treatment: the recurrent emphasis in mass media on predatory paedophiles and the 'different', evil and perverted nature of child abusers obscures an investigative focus on the pervasive, ordinary nature of child abuse within extended family networks. Somehow, it is much safer to pretend that child abuse is a special kind of problem that requires special treatment which most caring professionals cannot undertake. At a broader level, an exclusively psychotherapeutic focus on child abuse and the psychopathology of abusers risks deflecting attention from the way in which young persons and children are increasingly commodified and sexualized in media representations and marketing initiatives in the service of profit.

In a discussion on therapy with refugee families and the conflict in the former Yugoslavia, Papadopoulos and Hildebrand (1997) comment on the difficulties therapists and others have in conceptualizing warfare in relation to our normal lives:

> Despite the fact that millions of people's lives have been affected by war and its consequences, we have not yet found an appropriate way of recognising its place in the life-cycle. After each military conflict, there seems to be a recurrence of optimism that the world will finally settle into a more peaceful mode; yet, time and time again these expectations have been shattered by new outbreaks of hostility . . . It seems that there is a protective function in human beings which enables us to 'forget' painful memories of war and react with the wrath of naive ignorance when conflicts recur. It is as if humanity needs to keep cleansing itself from the horrors of war by constantly 'forgetting' them and thus renewing its virginal innocence.
>
> (Papadopoulos and Hildebrand 1997: 208–9)

Papadopolous and Hildebrand also suggest that the formation of 'specialist care industries' (such as therapy services for war refugees) constitutes part of the communal defensive denial of the normal horrors of war. This allows suffering to be thought about as something marginal to ordinary existence, split off into specialist services for exceptional circumstances. In these terms, the continuing failure of therapists to formulate a theoretical model and therapeutic theory of change regarding war suffering, which is not framed in terms of a 'pathology and deficit paradigm' (Papadopoulos and Hildebrand 1997: 209), can be understood partly as a collective defence against the existential horror of humanity's recurrent conflicts. However, as Santayana (1905) noted, those who cannot remember the past are condemned to repeat it.

Conclusion

These may seem overly pessimistic remarks with which to conclude this book. We need to reiterate that defences should not be understood as problematic *per se*; and this applies just as much to the idea of psychotherapy and counselling as a defensive structure in society, with its own defensive structures in its institutions, as it does in individual therapy. Psychotherapy may play a useful part in mediating and processing dangers experienced both by society and by individuals, particularly if this is part of an ongoing dialogue both with the wider community and in therapy itself. We suggest this is more likely if psychotherapists remain as curious about their own individual and collective defensive processes as they are about barriers, defences and resistance in their client, cultivating an awareness of the biases and vulnerabilities that shape both theory and practice.

References

Alexander, J. and Parsons, B. (1982) *Functional Family Therapy*. Monterey, CA: Brooks Cole.

Altschuler, J. (1997) *Working with Chronic Illness*. Basingstoke: Macmillan.

Andersen, T. (1990) *The Reflecting Team*. Broadstairs: Borgmann.

Anderson, H. (1997) *Conversation, Language and Possibilities*. New York: Basic Books.

Anderson, H. (2001) Postmodern collaborative and person-centred therapies: what would Carl Rogers say?, *Journal of Family Therapy*, 23(4): 339–60.

Andrews, B. (1995) Bodily shame as a mediator between abusive experiences and depression, *Journal of Abnormal Psychology*, 104: 277–85.

Aponte, H. (1985) The negotiation of values in therapy, *Family Process*, 24: 323–38.

Asen, E. (2002) Integrative therapy from a systemic perspective, in J. Holmes and A. Bateman (eds) *Integration in Psychotherapy*. Oxford: Oxford University Press.

Bannister, D. (1983) The internal politics of psychotherapy, in D. Pilgrim (ed.) *Psychology and Psychotherapy*. London: Routledge and Kegan Paul.

Beck, A.T. and Freeman, A. (1990) *Cognitive Therapy of Personality Disorders*. New York: Guilford.

Beck, A.T., Rush, A.J., Shaw, B.F. and Emery, G. (1979) *Cognitive Therapy of Depression*. New York: Wiley.

Beck, J. (1996) *Cognitive Therapy: Basics and Beyond*. New York: Guilford.

Bennett, P.L. (ed.) (2003) Ethical issues: whose interests?, *DECP Debate*, 105: 13–15.

Bentovim, A. (1992) *Trauma-Organised Systems*. London: Karnac.

Bergman, J. (1985) *Fishing for Barracuda*. New York: Norton.

Berman, E. and Segal, R. (1982) The captive client, *Psychotherapy, Research and Practice*, 19: 31–6.

Bernardez, T. (1991) Adolescent resistance and the maladies of women, in

C. Gilligan, A.G. Rogers and D.L. Tolman (eds) *Women, Girls and Psychotherapy: Reframing Resistance*. New York: Harrington Park Press.

Bhugra, D. and Davies, D. (2003) *Models of Psychopathology*. Maidenhead: Open University Press.

Billig, M. (1999) *Freudian Repression*. Cambridge: Cambridge University Press.

Billig, M. (2002) Freud and the language of humour, *The Psychologist*, 15(9): 452–5.

Bion, W.R. (1977) *Seven Servants*. New York: Jason Aronson.

Bloch, S. and Reddaway, P. (1977) *Psychiatric Terror: How Soviet Psychiatry Is Used to Suppress Dissent*. New York: Basic Books.

Bollas, C. and Sundelson, D. (1995) *The New Informants*. London: Karnac.

Borkovec, T.D., Shadick, R. and Hopkins, M. (1990) The nature of normal and pathological worry, in R. Rapee and D.H. Barlow (eds) *Chronic Anxiety and Generalized Anxiety Disorder*. New York: Plenum.

Boscolo, L. and Bertrando, P. (1993) *The Times of Time*. New York: Norton.

Boscolo, L., Cecchin, G., Hoffman, L. and Penn, P. (1987) *Milan Systemic Family Therapy*. New York: Basic Books.

Boss, M. (1967) *Psychoanalysis and Daseinanalysis* (trans. L.B. Lefebvre). New York: Basic Books.

Bowlby, J. (1988) *A Secure Base*. London: Hogarth Press.

Braun, B.G. (ed.) (1986) *Treatment of Multiple Personality Disorder*. Washington, DC: American Psychiatric Press.

Brewin, C.R. (1997) Psychological defences and the distortion of meaning, in M. Power and C.R. Brewin (eds) *The Transformation of Meaning in Psychological Therapies*. Chichester: Wiley.

Brinich, P.M. and Shelley, C. (2002) *The Self and Personality Structure*. Buckingham: Open University Press.

Brown, J. and Mowbray, R. (1994) Primal integration, in D. Jones (ed.) *Innovative Therapy*. Buckingham: Open University Press.

Bruch, M. and Bond, F. (eds) (1998) *Beyond Diagnosis*. Chichester: Wiley.

Bruner, J. (1986) *Actual Minds, Possible Worlds*. London: Harvard University Press.

Bruner, J. (1990) *Acts of Meaning*. London: Harvard University Press.

Bugental, J. (ed.) (1967) *Challenges of Humanistic Psychology*. New York: McGraw-Hill.

Bugental, J. and Bugental, E.K. (1984) A fate worse than death: the fear of change, *Psychotherapy*, 21: 543–9.

Burman, E., Aitken, G., Alldred, P., Allwood, R., Billington, T., Goldberg, B., Gordo Lopez, A.J., Heenan, C., Marks, D. and Warner, S. (1996) *Psychology, Discourse, Practice*. London: Taylor and Francis.

Burr, V. (1995) *An Introduction to Social Constructionism*. London: Routledge.

Burton, M. and Davey, T. (1996) The psychodynamic paradigm, in R. Woolfe and W. Dryden (eds) *Handbook of Counselling Psychology*. London: Sage.

Byng-Hall, J. (1995) *Re-writing Family Scripts*. London: Guilford.

Cade, B. and O'Hanlon, W.H. (1993) *A Brief Guide to Brief Therapy*. New York: Norton.

Campbell, D. (2000) *The Socially Constructed Organization*. London: Karnac.

Carey, M. and Russell, S. (2002) Externalising: commonly asked questions, *International Journal of Narrative Therapy and Community Work*, 2: 76–84.

Carr, A. (2000) *Family Therapy*. Chichester: Wiley.

Carroll, M. (1996) *Counselling Supervision*. London: Cassell.

Casement, P. (1985) *On Learning from the Patient*. London: Routledge.

Casement, P. (1990) *Further Learning from the Patient*. London: Routledge.

Cassidy, J. and Shaver, P.R. (eds) (1999) *Handbook of Attachment*. New York: Guilford.

Cecchin, G., Lane, G. and Ray, W. (1992) *Irreverence*. London: Karnac.

Cixous, H. and Clement, C. (1986) *The Newly Born Woman*. Manchester: Manchester University Press.

Clark, R.W. (1980) *The Man and the Cause*. London: Weidenfeld and Nicolson.

Cohen, S. (2001) *States of Denial: Knowing about Atrocities and Suffering*. Cambridge: Polity Press.

Collins, D. (2002) *Organisational Change: Sociological Perspectives*. London: Routledge.

Cornish, U. (1998) Death of a pupil in school, in P. Sutcliffe, G. Tufnell and U. Cornish (eds) *Working with the Dying and Bereaved*. London: Macmillan.

Cox, M. (1974) The psychotherapist's anxiety, *British Journal of Criminology*, 14: 1–17.

Cox, M. (1996) A supervisor's view, in C. Cordess and M. Cox, *Forensic Psychotherapy*. London: Jessica Kingsley.

Crane, D.R. and Hafen, M. (2002) Meeting the needs of evidence-based practice in family therapy, *Journal of Family Therapy*, 24: 113–24.

Cronen, V. and Pearce, B. (1985) Toward an explanation of how the Milan method works, in D. Campbell and R. Draper (eds) *Applications of Systemic Family Therapy*. London: Grune and Stratton.

Cunningham, R. (1991) When is a pervert not a pervert?, *British Journal of Psychotherapy*, 8: 48–70.

Danvaloo, H. (1987) Intensive short term dynamic psychotherapy with highly resistant depressed patients. Part I: restructuring the ego's regressive defences, *International Journal of Short Term Psychotherapy*, 2(2): 99–132.

Danvaloo, H. (1990) *Unlocking the Unconscious*. New York: Wiley.

Davy, J. (2002a) Discursive reflections on a research agenda for clinical supervision, *Psychology and Psychotherapy*, 75(2): 221–38.

Davy, J. (2002b) Personal therapy, in R. Bor and S. Palmer (eds) *A Beginner's Guide to Training in Counselling and Psychotherapy*. London: Sage.

Davy, J. (2003) Dead but not forgotten? A self-reflexive commentary on the death of resistance, *Counselling Psychology Review*, 18(1): 12–19.

de Shazer, S. (1984) The death of resistance, *Family Process*, 23(1): 79–93.

de Shazer, S. (1988) *Clues*. New York: Norton.

de Shazer, S. (1994) *Words Were Originally Magic*. New York: Norton.

Department of Health (2001) *Treatment Choice in Psychological Therapies and Counselling*. London: HMSO.

Dolan, Y.M. (1991) *Resolving Sexual Abuse*. London: Norton.

Down, G., Gorell Barnes, G. and McCann, D. (2000) Gender and systemic supervision, in G. Gorell Barnes, G. Down and D. McCann (eds) *Systemic Supervision*. London: Jessica Kingsley.

Dryden, W. (1990) *Rational-Emotive Counselling in Action*. London: Sage.

Dryden, W. and Trower, P. (eds) (1989) *Cognitive Psychotherapy: Stasis and Change*. London: Cassell.

Duncan, B.L. and Miller, S.D. (2000) The client's theory of change, *Journal of Psychotherapy Integration*, 10: 169–88.

Edwards, D. and Jacobs, M. (2003) *Conscious and Unconscious*. Buckingham: Open University Press.

Elliott, R. (1998) A guide to the empirically supported treatments controversy. *Psychotherapy Research*, 8: 115–25.

Engel, G. (1977) The need for a new medical model, *Science*, 196: 129–36.

Erdelyi, M.H. (1990) Repression, reconstruction and defense, in J.L. Singer (ed.) *Repression and Dissociation*. Chicago: University of Chicago Press.

Fairbairn, W.R.D. (1952) *Psychoanalytic Studies of the Personality*. London: Tavistock.

Falicov, C. (1995) Training to think culturally, *Family Process*, 34(4): 373–89.

Feltham, C. (2000) Counselling supervision, in B. Lawton and C. Feltham (eds) *Taking Supervision Forward*. London: Sage.

Ferenczi, S. (1932) Confusion of tongues between adults and the child (trans. J.M. Masson and M. Loring), in J.M. Masson (1985) *The Assault on Truth*. Harmondsworth: Penguin.

Ferenczi, S. (1988) *The Clinical Diary of Sandor Ferenczi* (ed. J. Dupont). Cambridge, MA: Harvard University Press.

Ferreira, A.J. (1963) Family myths and homeostasis, *Archives of General Psychiatry*, 9: 457–63.

Finkelhor, D. (1984) *Child Sexual Abuse*. New York: Free Press.

Flaskas, C. and Perlesz, A. (eds) (1996) *The Therapeutic Relationship in Systemic Therapy*. London: Karnac.

Folkman, S., Lazarus, R.S., Dunkel-Schetter, C., Delongis, A. and Gruen, R. (1986) The dynamics of a stressful encounter, *Journal of Personality and Social Psychology*, 50: 992–1003.

Fonagy, P. (2001) Attachment Theory and Psychoanalysis. New York: Other Press.

Fonagy, P., Gergely, G., Jurist, E. and Target, M. (2002) *Affect Regulation, Mentalization and the Development of the Self*. New York: Other Press.

Fonagy, P. and Target, M. (1997) Attachment and reflective function: their role in self-organization, *Development and Psychopathology*, 35(2): 231–57.

Forrester, J. (1990) *The Seductions of Psychoanalysis*. Cambridge: Cambridge University Press.

Foucault, M. (1965) *Madness and Civilization*. New York: Random House.

Foucault, M. (1977) *Discipline and Punish*. London: Allen Lane.

Foucault, M. (1984) *The History of Sexuality, Volume 1*. London: Peregrine Books.

Fransella, F. (1989) Obstacles to change and the reconstruing process: a personal construct view, in W. Dryden and P. Trower (eds) *Cognitive Psychotherapy: Stasis and Change*. London: Cassell.

Fransella, F. (1993) The construct of resistance in psychotherapy, in L. Leitner and N. Dunnett (eds) *Critical Issues in Personal Construct Psychotherapy*. Malabar, FL: Krieger.

Fransella, F. (2003) *International Handbook of Personal Construct Psychology*. Chichester: Wiley.

Fredericks, T. (2003) Recreating our community – memory, restitution and action, *International Journal of Narrative Therapy and Community Work*, 1: 66–9.

French, W.L. and Bell, C.H. (1999) *Organizational Development*. Englewood Cliffs, NJ: Prentice Hall.

Freud, A. (1936) *The Ego and the Mechanisms of Defence*. London: Hogarth.

Freud, S. (1905a) Analysis of a phobia in a five year old boy ('Little Hans'). Penguin Freud Library Volume 8. Harmondsworth: Penguin.

Freud, S. (1905b) Fragment of an analysis of a case of hysteria ('Dora'). Penguin Freud Library Volume 8. Harmondsworth: Penguin.

Freud, S. (1905c) *Jokes and Their Relation to the Unconscious*. Penguin Freud Library, Volume 6. Harmondsworth: Penguin.

Freud, S. (1905d) *Three Essays on the Theory of Sexuality*. Standard Edition, Volume 7. London: Virago.

Freud, S. (1910) *Five Lectures on Psychoanalysis*. Standard Edition, Volume 11. London: Virago.

Freud, S. (1911) *The Schreber Case*. London: Penguin Classics.

Freud, S. (1914) *Remembering, Repeating and Working Through*. Standard Edition, Volume 12. London: Virago.

Freud, S. (1915) *Repression*. Penguin Freud Library, Volume 11. Harmondsworth: Penguin.

Freud, S. (1920) *Beyond the Pleasure Principle*. Penguin Freud Library, Volume 11. Harmondsworth: Penguin.

Freud, S. (1930) *Civilisation and Its Discontents*. London: Penguin Classics.

Freud, S. and Breuer, J. (1895) *Studies on Hysteria*. Penguin Freud Library, Volume 3. Harmondsworth: Penguin.

Frosh, S. (1991) *Identity Crisis*. London: Macmillan.

Frosh, S. (1997) *For and Against Psychoanalysis*. London: Routledge.

Garland, A. (2001) Reclaiming the rubbish – a study of projective mechanisms, *Psychodynamic Counselling*, 7(2): 177–85.

Gaylin, N.L. (1993) Person-centred family therapy, in D. Brazier (ed.) *Beyond Carl Rogers*. London: Constable.

Geertz, C. (1973) Thick description: towards an interpretive theory of culture, in C. Geertz, *The Interpretation of Cultures*. New York: Basic Books.

Geertz, C. (1983) *Local Knowledge: Further Essays in Interpretive Anthropology*. New York: Basic Books.

Gendlin, E. (1981) *Focusing*. New York: Bantam Books.

Gergen, K.J. (1991) *The Saturated Self*. New York: Basic Books.

Gilbert, P. (1992) *Depression: The Evolution of Powerlessness*. Hove: Psychology Press.

Gilbert, P. (1995) Biopsychosocial approaches and evolutionary theory as aids to integration in clinical psychology and psychotherapy, *Clinical Psychology and Psychotherapy*, 2: 135–56.

Gilbert, P. (1998) Evolutionary psychopathology: why isn't the mind better designed than it is?, *British Journal of Medical Psychology*, 71: 353–73.

Gilbert, P. (2000) Varieties of submissive behaviour as forms of social defence, in L. Sloman and P. Gilbert (eds) *Subordination and Defeat*. Totowa, NJ: Lawrence Erlbaum.

Gilbert, P. and Allan, S. (1998) The role of defeat and entrapment (arrested flight) in depression, *Psychological Medicine*, 28: 584–97.

Gilbert, P. and Bailey, K.G. (eds) (2000) *Genes on the Couch: Explorations in Evolutionary Psychotherapy*. Hove: Brunner-Routledge.

Gilligan, C. (1982) *In a Different Voice*. Cambridge, MA: Harvard University Press.

Gilligan, C., Rogers, A.G. and Tolman, D.L. (eds) (1991) *Women, Girls and Psychotherapy: Reframing Resistance*. New York: Harrington Park Press.

Grant, J. and Crawley, J. (2002) *Transference and Projection*. Buckingham: Open University Press.

Greenberg, J.R. and Mitchell, S.A. (1983) *Object Relations in Psychoanalytic Theory*. Cambridge, MA: Harvard University Press.

Greenberg, L.S. and Pinsof, W.M. (1986) Process research, in L.S. Greenberg and W.M. Pinsof (eds) *The Psychotherapeutic Process: A Research Handbook*. New York: Guilford Press.

Griffiths, M. (2003) Terms of engagement: reaching hard to reach adolescents, *Young Minds Magazine*, 62: 23–6.

Guilfoyle, M. (2002) Rhetorical processes in therapy, *Journal of Family Therapy*, 24(3): 298–316.

Guntrip, H. (1968) *Schizoid Phenomena, Object Relations and the Self*. London: Hogarth Press.

Haines, G. (2000) Supervising practitioners working with people with anti-social personality disorder, in B. Lawton and C. Feltham (eds) *Taking Supervision Forward*. London: Sage.

Haley, J. (1963) *Strategies of Psychotherapy*. New York: Grune and Stratton.

Haley, J. (1985) *Conversations with Erickson*, three volumes. New York: Norton.

Haley, J. (1996) *Learning and Teaching Therapy*. New York: Guilford.

Harari, E. (1995) The longest shadow, *Australian and New Zealand Journal of Family Therapy*, 16: 11–13.

Harré, R. (1998) *The Singular Self*. London: Sage.

Henggeler, S.W. (1999) Multisystemic therapy: an overview of clinical procedures, outcomes and policy implications, *Child Psychology and Psychiatry Review*, 4(1): 2–10.

Hildebrand, J. (1998) *Bridging the Gap: A Training Module in Personal and Professional Development*. London: Karnac.

Hill, J., Fonagy, P., Safier, E. and Sargent, J. (2003) The ecology of attachment in the family, *Family Process*, 42(2): 205–22.

Hoffman, L. (1993) *Exchanging Voices*. London: Karnac.

Holmes, D.S. and Urie, R.G. (1975) Effects of preparing children for psychotherapy, *Journal of Consulting and Clinical Psychology*, 43: 311–18.

Holmes, J. (2001) *The Search for the Secure Base*. Hove: Brunner-Routledge.

Holmes, J. and Bateman, A. (1995) *An Introduction to Psychoanalysis*. Routledge: London.

Holmes, J. and Bateman, A. (eds) (2002) *Integration in Psychotherapy*. Oxford: Oxford University Press.

Horney, K. (1945) *Our Inner Conflicts*. London: Norton.

Horvath, A.O. and Greenberg, L. (1986) Process research, in L.S. Greenberg and W.M. Pinsof (eds) *The Psychotherapeutic Process: A Research Handbook*. New York: Guilford Press.

House, R. (2003) *Therapy Beyond Modernity*. London: Karnac.

Hoyt, M.F. (1995) *Brief Therapy and Managed Care*. San Fransisco: Jossey-Bass.

Illich, I. (1975) *Medical Nemesis*. London: Calder and Boyars.

Jackson, V. (2002) In our own voice: African-American stories of oppression, survival and recovery in mental health systems, *International Journal of Narrative Therapy and Community Work*, 2: 11–31.

Jacobs, M. (1995) *D.W. Winnicott*. London: Sage.

Jacobs, M. (1996) *In Search of Supervision*. Buckingham: Open University Press.

Jacobs, M. (2003) *Sigmund Freud*, 2nd edn. London: Sage.

Janov, A. (1973) *The Primal Scream*. London: Abacus.

Jenkins, A. (1990) *Invitations to Responsibility: The Therapeutic Engagement of Men who Are Violent and Abusive*. Adelaide: Dulwich Centre Publications.

Jenkins, P. (1997) *Counselling, Psychotherapy and the Law*. London: Sage.

Judd, D. (1989) *Give Sorrow Words: Working with a Dying Child*. London: Free Association Books.

Kaberry, S. (2000) Abuse in supervision, in B. Lawton and C. Feltham (eds) *Taking Supervision Forward*. London: Sage.

Karen, B.P. and Bos, G.V. (1981) *Psychotherapy of Schizophrenia*. New York: Jason Aronson.

Kazdin, A. *et al.* (1997) Barriers to treatment participation scale, *Journal of Child Psychology and Psychiatry*, 38(8): 1051–62.

Kelly, G. (1955) *The Psychology of Personal Constructs*. New York: Norton.

Khandwalla, P.N. (1977) *The Design of Organizations*. New York: Harcourt, Brace, Jovanovich.

Kitwood, T. (1997) *Dementia Reconsidered*. Buckingham: Open University Press.

Kitzinger, C. (1993) Depoliticising the personal: a feminist slogan in feminist therapy, *Woman's Studies International Forum*, 16(5): 487–96.

Kitzinger, C. and Perkins, R. (1993) *Changing Our Minds: Lesbian Feminism and Psychology*. London: Onlywomen Press.

Klein, M. (1946) Notes on some schizoid mechanisms, in J. Mitchell (ed., 1986) *The Selected Melanie Klein*. Harmondsworth: Penguin.

Klein, M. (1952) The origin of transference, *International Journal of Psychoanalysis*, 33: 433–8.

Kogan, S.M. (1998) The politics of making meaning: discourse analysis of a 'postmodern' interview, *Journal of Family Therapy*, 20(3): 229–52.

Krause, I.B. (2002) Uncertainty, risk-taking and ethics in therapy, in B. Mason and A. Sawyerr (eds) *Exploring the Unsaid*. London: Karnac.

Kriegman, D. (2000) Evolutionary psychoanalysis, in P. Gilbert and K.G. Bailey (eds) *Genes on the Couch*. Hove: Brunner-Routledge.

Kutchins, H. and Kirk, S.A. (1999) *Making US Crazy*. London: Constable.

Ladany, N., Hill, C.E., Corbett, M. and Nutt, E.A. (1996) Nature, extent and importance of what psychotherapy trainees do not disclose to their supervisors, *Journal of Counseling Psychology*, 43(1): 10–24.

Laing, R.D. (1960) *The Divided Self*. London: Tavistock.

Laing, R.D. (1967) *The Politics of Experience/The Bird of Paradise*. Harmondsworth: Penguin.

Laing, R.D. and Esterson, A. (1964) *Sanity, Madness and the Family*. Harmondsworth: Penguin.

Lang, P. and McAdam, E. (1997) Narrative-ating: future dreams in present living, *Human Systems*, 8(1): 3–12.

Langs, R. (1994) *Doing Supervision and Being Supervised*. New York: Aronson.

Larson, M. (1977) *The Rise of Professionalism*. Berkeley: University of California Press.

Law, I. (1998) Attention deficit disorders: therapy with a shoddily built construct, in S. Madigan and I. Law (eds) *Praxis*. Vancouver: Yaletown Family Therapy.

Law, I. (1999) A discursive approach to therapy with men, in I. Parker (ed.) *Deconstructing Psychotherapy*. London: Sage.

Lawton, B. (1996) A very exposing affair. Explorations in counsellors' supervisory relationships. Unpublished MA thesis, University of Leeds.

Leahy, R.L. (2001) *Overcoming Resistance in Cognitive Therapy*. New York: Guilford.

Legg, C. and Stagaki, P. (2002) How to be a postmodernist: a user's guide to postmodern rhetorical practices, *Journal of Family Therapy*, 24(4): 385–401.

Lemma, A. (1996) *Introduction to Psychopathology*. London: Sage.

Levine, R.V. and Bartlett, C. (1984) Pace of life, punctuality and coronary heart disease in six countries, *Journal of Cross-cultural Psychology*, 15: 233–55.

Lietaer, G. (1984) Unconditional positive regard: a controversial basic attitude in client-centred therapy, in R. Levant and J. Shlien (eds) *Client-centred Therapy and the Person-centred Approach*. New York: Praeger.

Linehan, M. (1993) *Cognitive-behavioural Treatment of Borderline Personality Disorder*. New York: Guilford Press.

Liotti, G. (1989) Resistance to change in cognitive psychotherapy: theoretical remarks from a constructivist point of view, in W. Dryden and P. Trower (eds) *Cognitive Psychotherapy: Stasis and Change*. London: Cassell.

Loftus, E.F., Garry, M. and Feldman, J. (1994) Forgetting sexual trauma: what does it mean when 38% forget?, *Journal of Consulting and Clinical Psychology*, 62: 1177–81.

McCann, D., Gorell Barnes, G. and Down, G. (2000) Sex and sexuality, in G. Gorell Barnes, G. Down and D. McCann (eds) *Systemic Supervision.* London: Jessica Kingsley.

McDougall, J. (1986) *Theatres of the Mind. Illusion and Truth on the Psycho-analytic Stage.* New York: Basic Books.

Mace, C., Moorey, S. and Roberts, B. (eds) (2001) *Evidence in the Psychological Therapies.* Hove: Brunner-Routledge.

McLeod, J. (1996) The humanistic paradigm, in R. Woolfe and W. Dryden (eds) *Handbook of Counselling Psychology.* London: Sage.

McLeod, J. (1997) *Narrative and Psychotherapy.* London: Sage.

McLeod, J. (1999) Counselling as a social process, *Counselling,* 10(3): 217–22.

McNamee, S. and Gergen, K.J. (1992) *Therapy as Social Construction.* London: Sage.

McNamee, S., Gergen, K.J. and Associates (1999) *Relational Responsibility.* London: Sage.

Macpherson, W. (1999) *The Stephen Lawrence Inquiry.* London: HMSO.

Mahoney, M.J. (1991) *Human Change Processes.* New York: Basic Books.

Main, M., Kaplan, N. and Cassidy, J. (1985) Security in infancy, childhood and adulthood: a move to the level of representation, *Monographs of the Society for Research in Child Development,* 50 (serial no. 209): 66–106.

Mair, M. (1989) *Between Psychology and Psychotherapy: A Poetics of Experience.* London: Routledge.

Malan, D. (1976) *The Frontier of Brief Psychotherapy.* New York: Plenum.

Maslow, A. (1968) *Towards a Psychology of Being.* New York: Van Nostrand Reinhold.

Mason, B. (1993) Towards positions of safe uncertainty, *Human Systems,* 4: 189–200.

Mason, B. and Sawyerr, A. (2002) *Exploring the Unsaid.* London: Karnac.

Masson, J. (1985a) *The Assault on Truth: Freud's Suppression of the Seduction Theory.* Harmondsworth: Penguin.

Masson, J. (ed.) (1985b) *The Complete Letters of Sigmund Freud to Wilhelm Fliess.* Cambridge, MA: Belknap Press.

Masson, J. (1993) *Against Therapy.* London: HarperCollins.

Mearns, D. and Thorne, B. (1988) *Person-centred Counselling in Action.* London: Sage.

Menzies-Lyth, I.E.P. (1960) *The Functioning of Social Systems as a Defence against Anxiety.* London: Tavistock.

Miller, S.D., Duncan, B.L. and Hubble, M.A. (1997) *Escape from Babel.* London: Norton.

Miller, W.R. and Rollnick, S. (1991) *Motivational Interviewing.* New York: Guilford Press.

Minuchin, S. (1974) *Families and Family Therapy.* London: Tavistock.

Minuchin, S. (1998) Where is the family in narrative family therapy?, *Journal of Marital and Family Therapy,* 24: 397–403.

Mitchell, S.A. and Black, M.J. (1995) *Freud and Beyond.* New York: Basic Books.

Mowbray, R. (1995) *The Case against Psychotherapy Registration*. London: TransMarginal Press.

Nesse, R. (1990) The evolutionary functions of repression and the ego defences, *Journal of the American Academy of Psychoanalysis*, 18: 260–85.

Newth, S. and Rachman, S. (2001) The concealment of obsessions, *Behaviour Research and Therapy*, 37: 347–68.

Obholzer, A. and Roberts, V.Z. (eds) (1994) *The Unconscious at Work*. London: Routledge.

O'Hanlon, W.H. and Beadle, S. (1997) *A Field-guide to Possibilityland*. London: BT Press.

Owen, I.R. (1995) Power, boundaries, intersubjectivity, *British Journal of Medical Psychology*, 68: 97–107.

Owusu-Bempah, K. (2002) Culture, self, and cross-ethnic therapy, in B. Mason and A. Sawyerr (eds) *Exploring the Unsaid*. London: Karnac.

Papadopoulos, R.K. and Hildebrand, J. (1997) Is home where the heart is? Narratives of oppositional discourses in refugee families, in R.K. Papadopoulos and J. Byng-Hall (eds) *Multiple Voices: Narrative in Systemic Family Psychotherapy*. London: Duckworth.

Parker, I., Georgaca, E., Harper, D., McLaughlin, T. and Stowell-Smith, M. (1995) *Deconstructing Psychopathology*. London: Sage.

Patterson, C.H. (1984) Empathy, warmth and genuineness in psychotherapy: a review of reviews, *Psychotherapy*, 21(4): 431–8.

Patton, M.J. and Kivlighan, D.M. (1997) Relevance of the supervisor alliance to the counselling alliance and to treatment adherence in counselling training, *Journal of Counselling Psychology*, 44(1): 108–15.

Penn, P. (1985) Feed-forward, *Family Process*, 24(3): 299–310.

Perkins, R. (1991) Therapy for lesbians? The case against, *Feminism and Psychology*, 1(3): 325–38.

Perron, R. (1999) Reflections on psychoanalytic research problems, in P. Fonagy, H. Kaechele, R. Krause, E. Jones and R. Perron (eds) *An Open Door Review of Outcome Studies in Psychoanalysis*. London: UCL Psychoanalysis Unit.

Persons, J. (1989) *Cognitive Therapy in Practice*. New York: Norton.

Pilgrim, D. (1988) Psychotherapy and British special hospitals: a case of failure to thrive, *Free Associations*, 11: 58–72.

Pilgrim, D. (1992) Psychotherapy and political evasions, in W. Dryden and C. Feltham (eds) *Psychotherapy and Its Discontents*. Buckingham: Open University Press.

Pilgrim, D. (1997) *Psychotherapy and Society*. London: Sage.

Plunkett, J. (1984) Parents' treatment expectations and attrition from a child psychiatric service, *Journal of Clinical Psychology*, 40: 372–7.

Pollner, M. and Wikler, L. (1985) The social construction of unreality, *Family Process*, 24(2): 241–59.

Prochaska, J. and DiClemente, C. (1992) *The Transtheoretical Approach to Therapy*. New York: Basic Books.

Rank, O. (1929) *The Trauma of Birth*. London: Routledge.

Raval, H. (1996) A systemic perspective on working with interpreters, *Clinical Child Psychology and Psychiatry*, 1: 29–43.

Raval, H. (2000) Therapists' experiences of working with interpreters. Unpublished DClinPsych thesis, University of Surrey.

Red Horse, J. (1997) Traditional American Indian family systems, *Families, Systems and Health*, 15(3): 243–50.

Reich, W. (1945) *Character Analysis*. New York: Orgone Institute Press.

Richards, G. (2002) A risky balance: striving to merge professional white issues and personal black issues, in B. Mason and A. Sawyerr (eds) *Exploring the Unsaid*. London: Karnac.

Ridley, C.R. (1995) *Overcoming Unintentional Racism in Counselling and Therapy*. London: Sage.

Roberts, G. (1991) Delusional belief systems and meaning in life: a preferred reality?, *British Journal of Psychiatry*, 159 (suppl. 14): 19–28.

Rogers, A.G. (1991) A feminist poetics of psychotherapy, in C. Gilligan, A.G. Rogers and D.L. Tolman (eds) *Women, Girls and Psychotherapy: Reframing Resistance*. New York: Harrington Park Press.

Rogers, C.R. (1951) *Client-centred Therapy*. Boston: Houghton Mifflin.

Rogers, C.R. (1957) The necessary and sufficient conditions of therapeutic personality change, *Journal of Consulting Psychology*, 21: 95–103.

Rogers, C.R. (1961) *On Becoming a Person*. Boston: Houghton Mifflin.

Rogers, C.R. (1963) The actualizing tendency in relation to 'motives' and to consciousness, in M. Jones (ed.) *Nebraska Symposium on Motivation*. Lincoln: University of Nebraska.

Rogers, C.R. (1969) *Freedom to Learn*. Columbus, OH: Charles E. Merrill.

Rogers, C.R. (1978) *Carl Rogers on Personal Power*. London: Constable.

Rogers, C.R. (1989) Reflections of feelings and transference, in H. Kirschenbaum and V.L. Henderson (eds) *The Carl Rogers Reader*. London: Constable.

Rolland, J. (1995) *Families, Illness and Disability*. New York: Basic Books.

Rorty, R. (1979) *Philosophy and the Mirror of Nature*. Princeton, NJ: Princeton University Press.

Rosenfeld, H. (1987) *Impasse and Interpretation*. London: Routledge.

Rowan, J. and Jacobs, M. (2002) *Therapist's Use of Self*. Buckingham: Open University Press.

Ryle, A. (1990) *Cognitive-analytic Therapy: Active Participation in Change*. Chichester: Wiley.

Ryle, A. (1995) *Cognitive-analytic Therapy: Developments in Theory and Practice*. Chichester: Wiley.

Ryle, A. (1997) *Cognitive-analytic Therapy and Borderline Personality Disorder*. Chichester: Wiley.

Sackett, D.L., Rosenberg, W.M.C., Gray, J.A.M., Harnes, R.B. and Richardson, W.S. (1996) Evidence based medicine: what it is and what it isn't, *British Medical Journal*, 312: 71–2.

Safran, J.D. (1993) The therapeutic alliance rupture as a transtheoretical phenomenon: definitional and conceptual issues, *Journal of Psychotherapy Integration*, 3(1): 33–49.

Safran, J.D. and Segal, L.S. (1990) *Interpersonal Process in Cognitive Therapy*. New York: Basic Books.

Salkovskis, P.M. (1985) Obsessional-compulsive problems, *Behaviour Research and Therapy*, 23: 571–83.

Sampson, E. (1993) *Celebrating the Other*. San Fransisco: Westview Press.

Sandler, J. (1992) Reflections on some relations between psychoanalytic concepts and psychoanalytic practice, *International Journal of Psychoanalysis*, 73: 189–98.

Santayana, G. (1905) *The Life of Reason, Volume 1*. London: Scribner.

Sartre, J.P. ([1956] 1991) *Being and Nothingness* (trans. H. Barnes). London: Routledge.

Schafer, R. (1992) *Retelling a Life*. New York: Basic Books.

Schoenewolf, G. (1993) *Counterresistance*. London: Jason Aronson.

Schore, A.N. (1994) *Affect Regulation and the Origin of the Self*. Hillsdale, NJ: Lawrence Erlbaum Associates.

Segal, H. (1964) *Introduction to the Work of Melanie Klein*. London: Heinemann Medical Books.

Selekman, M. (2002) *Living on the Razor's Edge*. London: Norton.

Selvini-Palazzoli, M., Boscolo, L., Cecchin, G. and Prata, G. (1978) *Paradox and Counterparadox*. New York: Jason Aronson.

Selvini-Palazzoli, M., Boscolo, L., Cecchin, G. and Prata, G. (1980) The problem of the referring person, *Journal of Marital and Family Therapy*, 6: 3–9.

Shiang, J., Kjellander, C., Huang, K. and Bogumill, S. (1998) Developing cultural competency in clinical practice, *Clinical Psychology: Science and Practice*, 5(2): 182–210.

Shotter, J. and Gergen, K.J. (eds) (1989) *Texts of Identity*. London: Sage.

Simanowitz, V. and Pearce, P. (2003) *Personality Development*. Buckingham: Open University Press.

Skynner, R. (1989) *Institutes and How to Survive Them*. London: Methuen.

Sloman, L., Atkinson, L., Milligan, K. and Liotti, G. (2002) Attachment, social rank and affect regulation, *Family Process*, 41: 313–27.

Smail, D. (1996) *Getting by Without Psychotherapy*. London: HarperCollins.

Smith, G. (1993) *Systemic Approaches to Training in Child Protection*. London: Karnac.

Spinelli, E. (1994) *Demystifying Therapy*. London: Constable.

Spinelli, E. (1996) The existential-phenomenological paradigm, in R. Woolfe and W. Dryden (eds) *Handbook of Counselling Psychology*. London: Sage.

Spinelli, E. (2001) *The Mirror and the Hammer*. London: Continuum.

Steiner, J. (1994) Foreword, in M. Jackson and P. Williams, *Unimaginable Storms: a Search for Meaning in Psychosis*. London: Karnac.

Stern, D.N. (1998) *The Interpersonal World of the Infant*, 2nd edn. London: Karnac.

Strean, H. (1993) *Resolving Counter-Resistances in Psychotherapy*. New York: Brunner-Mazel.

Stroebe, E.J.W. and Stroebe, M.S. (1995) *Social Psychology and Health*. London: Brooks Cole.

Sturdee, P. (2001) Evidence, influence or evaluation? Fact and value in clinical science, in C. Mace, S. Moorey and B. Roberts (eds) *Evidence in the Psychological Therapies*. Hove: Brunner-Routledge.

Sullivan, H.S. (1953) *The Interpersonal Theory of Psychiatry*. New York: Norton.

Szasz, T. (1961) *The Myth of Mental Illness*. New York: Harper and Row.

Tarrier, N. and Calam, R. (2002) New developments in cognitive-behavioural case formulation, *Behavioural and Cognitive Psychotherapy*, 30: 311–28.

Thornton, E.M. (1999) Does the unconscious mind really exist?, in C. Feltham (ed.) *Controversies in Psychotherapy and Counselling*. London: Sage.

Triandis, H.C. (1995) *Individualism and Collectivism*. Boulder, CO: Westview Press.

Tudor, K. (2000) The case of the lost conditions, *Counselling*, February: 33–7.

Turner, V. (1969) *The Ritual Process*. New York: Cornell University Press.

Ussher, J. (1991) *Women's Madness: Misogyny or Mental Illness?* Hemel Hempstead: Harvester Wheatsheaf.

Vaillant, G.E. (1992) *Ego Mechanisms of Defense*. Washington, DC: American Psychiatric Association Press.

van Deurzen-Smith, E. (1988) *Existential Counselling in Practice*. London: Sage.

Van Marle, S. and Holmes, J. (2002) Supportive psychotherapy as an integrative psychotherapy, in J. Holmes and A. Bateman (eds) *Integration in Psychotherapy*. Oxford: Oxford University Press.

Vetere, A. (2001) Structural family therapy, *Child Psychology and Psychiatry Review*, 6(3): 133–9.

Viney, L.L. (1993) *Life Stories: Personal Construct Therapy with the Elderly*. Chichester: Wiley.

Volberda, H.E. (1999) *Building the Flexible Firm*. Oxford: Oxford University Press.

Vygotsky, L.S. (1962) *Thought and Language*. Cambridge, MA: MIT Press.

Vygotsky, L.S. (1978) *Mind in Society*. Cambridge, MA: Harvard University Press.

Waldegrave, C.T. (1990) Just therapy, *Dulwich Centre Newsletter*, 1: 5–46.

Walter, T. (2000) *On Bereavement*. Buckingham: Open University Press.

Watzlawick, P., Weakland, J.H. and Fisch, R. (1974) *Change*. London: Norton.

Webb, A. (2000) What makes it difficult for the supervisee to speak?, in B. Lawton and C. Feltham (eds) *Taking Supervision Forward*. London: Sage.

Webb, A. and Wheeler, S. (1998) How honest do counsellors dare to be in the supervisory relationship? An exploratory study, *British Journal of Guidance and Counselling*, 26: 509–24.

Weick, K.E. (1982) Management of organisational change among loosely coupled elements, in P.S. Goodman and Associates (eds) *Change in Organizations*. San Francisco: Jossey-Bass.

Weingarten, K. (ed.) (1995) *Cultural Resistance: Challenging Beliefs about Men, Women and Therapy*. New York: Harrington Park Press.

Wessely, S. (2001) Randomised controlled trials: the gold standard?, in C. Mace, S. Moorey and B. Roberts (eds) *Evidence in the Psychological Therapies*. Hove: Brunner-Routledge.

White, M. (1997) *Narratives of Therapist's Lives*. Adelaide: Dulwich Centre Publications.

White, M. (2001) Folk psychology and narrative practice, *Dulwich Centre Journal*, 2: 3–37.

White, M. (2002) Addressing personal failure, *International Journal of Narrative Therapy and Community Work*, 3: 33–76.

White, M. and Epston, D. (1990) *Narrative Means to Therapeutic Ends*. New York: Norton.

Wilber, K. (1980) *The Atman Project: A Transpersonal View of Human Development*. Wheaton, IL: Quest Books.

Wilson, J. (1998) *Child-focused Practice: A Collaborative Systemic Approach*. London: Karnac.

Winnicott, D.W. (1965) *The Maturational Process and the Facilitating Environment*. London: Hogarth Press.

Winnicott, D.W. (1975) Hate in the countertransference, in D.W. Winnicott, *Collected Papers*, 2nd edn. London: Tavistock.

Wittgenstein, L. (1958) *Philosophical Investigations*, 2nd edn (trans. G.E.M. Anscombe). Oxford: Blackwell.

Woolfe, R. and Dryden, W. (eds) (1996) *Handbook of Counselling Psychology*. London: Sage.

Worrell, M. (2002) Resistance is futile? An existential-phenomenological exploration of psychotherapists' experiences of 'encountering resistance' in psychotherapy. Unpublished PhD thesis, Regent's College/City University, London.

Yalom, I.D. (1980) *Existential Psychotherapy*. New York: Basic Books.

Yegdich, T. (1999) Lost in the crucible of supportive clinical supervision: supervision is not therapy, *Journal of Advanced Nursing*, 29(5): 1265–75.

Young, J.E. (1994) *Cognitive Therapy for Personality Disorders: A Schema-focused Approach*. Sarasota, FL: Professional Resource Exchange.

Zilbach, J. (1986) *Young Children in Family Therapy*. New York: Brunner-Mazel.

Index

THE SELF AND PERSONALITY STRUCTURE

Paul M. Brinich and Christopher Shelley

- What is the self and its relationship to personality theories?
- How do the central schools of psychotherapy conceptualize the self?

The *self* is a notoriously difficult and at times obscure concept that underpins and guides much psychotherapy theory and practice. The corollary concept of personality is fundamentally linked to the concept of the self and has provided theorists and researchers in psychology with a more coherent set of principles with which to explicate the personal and attributional aspects of the self. The authors come from two quite separate schools of depth psychology (psychoanalytic and Adlerian) and provide an overview of the self and how it is conceptualized across the psychotherapies within various theories of personality. In addition to outlining some of the philosophical and historical issues surrounding the notion of selfhood, the authors examine classical and developmental models of psychoanalytic thought that implicitly point to the idea of self. The authors also outline Kohut's psychoanalytic *self psychology* in addition to Adlerian and other post-Freudian, Jungian and post-Jungian, cognitive, humanistic, and existential contributions to the self and personality structure.

Contents
Introduction – The self and personality in context – Psychoanalytic perspectives on the self: classical models – Psychoanalytic perspectives on the self: developmental models – Kohut and self psychology – The social and interpersonal self in Adlerian and neo-Freudian theory – Jungian and post-Jungian perspectives on the self – Cognitive perspectives on the self – Humanistic and existential perspectives on the self – Conclusion – References – Index.

128pp   0 335 20563 1 (Paperback)   0 335 20564 X (Hardback)

MODELS OF PSYCHOPATHOLOGY

Dilys Davies and Dinesh Bhugra

Models and theories of psychopathology and their associated clinical practice do not represent scientific fact so much as a variation in perspective within psychopathology itself. Several favoured models exist within any society at a given time, and as well as changing historically over time, they also differ culturally between societies.
This book examines:

- the similarities, differences and points of integration in the main models of psychopathology
- how the theoretical conceptualizations underpinning these models are reflected in the theory and the clinical practice of different schools of psychotherapy
- how various models are used in everyday practice
- whether clinicians adhere to the rules of a given model or whether, in fact, there is more integration in practice than there appears to be in theoretical conceptualizations.

Models of Psychopathology is aimed at advanced undergraduates and postgraduate students of clinical psychology, counselling psychology, psychotherapy and counselling. It will also be of interest to therapy students in professional training courses and experienced clinicians who want to know more about this aspect of psychotherapy.

Contents
Series editor's preface – Introduction – Descriptive models – Psychoanalytical model – Behavioural model – Cognitive model – Humanistic model – Social model – Critique from a socio-cultural view – Conclusion – References – Index.

128pp   0 335 20822 3 (Paperback)   0 335 20823 1 (Hardback)

PERSONALITY DEVELOPMENT

Valerie Simanowitz and Peter Pearce

This book draws out the essence of a range of personality theories in a clear and accessible way, moving from the seminal works of Freud and other prominent analytical theorists, to the stage theories of Erikson and Levinson and the development of personality as it is viewed in existential and person-centred theory. The text:

- Highlights the salient points of different personality theories
- Critiques the theories
- Examines important aspects of personality development neglected by previous books on this topic such as spirituality and the development of racial identity and gender.

The book reflects strongly on the context from which the theories sprang and seeks to trace how this context has influenced the theorists and their disciples. It also highlights the similarities between the concepts and structure of many of the theories. The authors, both experienced counsellors and trainers, evaluate which elements of the theories can be useful to the work of the therapist in the twenty first century and give examples from their case work.

Personality Development is a valuable new resource for practitioners, lecturers and trainers as well as students of counselling, psychotherapy and psychology.

Contents
Series editor's preface – Preface – Psychoanalytic/psychodynamic developmental theories – The developmental theories of Erikson and Levinson – Personality development in person-centred theory – Existential approaches – Moral development – Feminist critiques of developmental theories – Cultural factors in personality development (with particular reference to black identity) – Transpersonal and psycho-spiritual psychology – Conclusion – References – Index.

172pp   0 335 20635 2 (Paperback)   0 335 20636 0 (Hardback)

CONSCIOUS AND UNCONSCIOUS
David Edwards and Michael Jacobs

All forms of psychotherapy deal with the limitations of our awareness. We have limited knowledge of our creative potential, of the details of our own behaviour, of our everyday emotional states, of what motivates us, and of the many factors within and around us which influence the decisions we make and the ways we act.

Some therapists, especially those influenced by Freud and Jung, speak of the 'unconscious', giving the unintended impression that it is a kind of realm or domain of activity. Others, reacting against the specifics of Freudian theory, shun the word 'unconscious' altogether. However, so limited is the reach of everyday awareness and such is the range of unconscious factors, that one way or another these limitations must somehow be spoken about, sometimes in metaphor, sometimes more explicitly.

This book offers a broad survey of psychotherapy discourses, including:

- The psychoanalytic
- The interpersonal
- The experiential
- The cognitive-behavioural
- The transpersonal

This book offers a comprehensive overview of the ways in which these discourses employ a rich variety of concepts to address the limits of our everyday consciousness.

Conscious and Unconscious is invaluable reading for all those interested in counselling and psychotherapy, including those in training, as well as for experienced therapists.

Contents
Series editor's preface – Preface and acknowledgements – Constructing and deconstructing the unconscious – Conscious and unconscious in historical perspective – Freud, Adler and Jung: contrasting perspectives on the psychology of the unconscious – The development of alternative discourses: Harry Stack Sullivan, Fritz Perls and Medard Boss – Evolving psychoanalytic discourses of the unconscious – Cognitive therapy, cognitive science and the cognitive unconscious – Invisible worlds, unconscious fields and the non-egoic core: evolving discourses of the transpersonal unconscious – Conscious and unconscious: the next hundred years – References – Index.

184pp   0 335 20949 1 (Paperback)   0 335 20950 5 (Hardback)

AN INTRODUCTION TO COUNSELLING
THIRD EDITION

John McLeod

This thoroughly revised and expanded version of the bestselling text, *An Introduction to Counselling*, provides a comprehensive introduction to the theory and practice of counselling and therapy. It is written in a clear, accessible style, covers all the core approaches to counselling, and takes a critical, questioning approach to issues of professional practice.

Placing each counselling approach in its social and historical context, the book also introduces a wide range of contemporary approaches, including narrative therapy, systemic, feminist and multicultural.

This third edition includes a new chapter on the important emerging approach of philosophical counselling, and a chapter on the counselling relationship, as well as expanded coverage of attachment theory, counselling on the internet, and solution-focused therapy. The text has been updated throughout, with additional illustrative vignettes and case studies.

Current, comprehensive and readable, with exhaustive references, *An Introduction to Counselling* is a classic introduction to its subject.

Contents
Preface – An introduction to counselling – The cultural and historical origins of counselling – Counselling theories: diversity and convergence – Themes and issues in the psychodynamic approach to counselling – From behaviourism to constructivism: the cognitive-behavioural approach to counselling – Theory and practice of the person-centred approach – Working with systems – Feminist approaches: the radicalization of counselling – Narrative approaches to counselling: working with stories – Multiculturalism as an approach to counselling – Philosophical counselling – The counselling relationship – The process of counselling – The politics of counselling: empowerment, control and difference – Morals, values and ethics in counselling practice – The organizational context of counselling – Alternative modes of delivery – The role of research in counselling and therapy – The skills and qualities of the effective counsellor – Training and supervision in counselling – Beyond an introduction: continuing the conversation – References – Index.

640pp   0 335 21189 5 (Paperback)